THE MYSTERY OF CHRIST

. . . and why we don't get it

Theology

The Mystery of Christ

. . . and why we don't get it

ROBERT FARRAR CAPON

WILLIAM B. EERDMANS PUBLISHING COMPANY
GRAND RAPIDS, MICHIGAN

Copyright © 1993 by Wm. B. Eerdmans Publishing Co.

255 Jefferson Ave. S.E., Grand Rapids, Mich. 49503

Printed in the United States of America

Reprinted 1998

Library of Congress Cataloging-in-Publication Data

Capon, Robert Farrar.

The mystery of Christ: . . . and why we don't get it /

Robert Farrar Capon.

p.   cm.

ISBN 0-8028-0121-8 (pbk.)

1. Salvation. 2. Mystery. I. Title.

BT751.2.C35   1993

234 — dc20   93-26653

CIP

Most of the citations of Scripture in this publication are from the New Revised Standard Version Bible, copyright © 1989 by the Division of Christian Education of the National Council of Churches of Christ in the U.S.A., and used by permission.

To my parents, who taught me to speak;
and my friends, who taught me to listen:

οὐδὲν ἄρα νῦν κατάκριμα τοῖς ἐν Χριστῷ Ἰησοῦ

There is therefore now no condemnation
for those who are in Christ Jesus.

Romans 8:1

Contents

ONE

Helen

Where this book is going, and how I propose to get it there, will become obvious by and by. Meanwhile, accepting T. S. Eliot's dictum that "all cases are unique, and very similar to others," let me begin with the first one that comes to mind.

❦   ❦

Helen was in her late forties — a writer, but with nothing published yet. I'd known her and her husband for some four years, but our conversations had been limited to a couple of coffee-hour chats after sermons I'd preached and one literary exchange while I was sitting next to her at a dinner party. When she phoned for an appointment, I automatically assumed the worst — namely, that I was about to be asked to read a work in progress.

I'm terrible about that. I never say no; but neither do I work up any enthusiasm for tackling the job. With enough embarrassing reminders, I may eventually get around to it; but most of the time the manuscript just drifts downward in the stack of things to do until the annual office-cleaning binge turns it up again. Then I feel bad as briefly as possible and let the downward drift take over once more. John Updike has the right idea. I read somewhere that he responds to all requests with a printed card itemizing the things he doesn't do. Not reading unsolicited manuscripts, as I recall, is at the top of his list: guilt finessed by boldness.

Anyway, when Helen arrived that Monday morning, she had with her an ominously large handbag and launched right into the subject of her novel, asking whether I thought taking it to an agent would be a good idea. Whatever my faults, I can at least spot a chance to land a manuscript in somebody else's lap; so I encouraged her, even coming up with a few names she might try for openers. Then, just as I was expecting her hand to go straight into the bag, she changed the subject abruptly.

"But that's not what I really came to talk about," she said.

Silence. I waited a bit and finally said, "All right. Next subject. What's up?"

"It's about my daughter. But it's also about me."

Silence again. Then she said, "I know I'm doing this badly, but I don't seem to know where to start. There's so much to it."

"Start with whatever's easiest for you to talk about," I suggested. "Obviously, it's all connected inside yourself. Just begin anywhere and go backwards and forwards. Eventually you'll get it all out."

"Okay," she said; "my daughter first — Barbara, that is, the nineteen-year-old. About four weeks ago, she was staying with some friends up at Snow Mountain, and she had a terrible accident. She'd been out skiing by herself and when she didn't come back after about three hours, the people she was staying with went out to look for her. When they found her, she was lying unconscious next to a tree. Apparently she'd lost control and hit the tree with her head and right shoulder. Anyway, they contacted the medics and got her to the hospital. Then they called my husband and me. To make a long story short, she had a broken shoulder and a very severe skull fracture. Ted and I flew right up, but she was in a coma and stayed that way for a week. The doctors didn't sound particularly hopeful at the outset, but when she came around after that week, they began to be more encouraging."

"How is she now?" I asked.

"Much better. No permanent damage, they say. But it was the worst scare I've ever had. I thought about all kinds of things. Like losing her altogether, or having her in a vegetative state for the rest of her life, or having her paralyzed."

She hesitated. Then she took a deep breath and went on rapidly.

"What I really want to talk to you about is something I did during that first week. For over a year now, I've been having an affair. I've always hated that word. It sounds so detached and masculine, which wasn't the way I felt about it at all. But anyway, back there in that first week, when everything looked so black, I made a promise to God — or maybe it was a bargain with God; I don't know — that if Barbara pulled through, I would end the affair. I suppose what I'm here for is to ask you whether, now that she's better, I really have to do something about the promise — make good on it, that is."

She stopped abruptly. I let a few beats go by, then asked her, "What do you *want* to do about it?"

"Why do you ask me that? If I knew what I wanted, I wouldn't be here, would I?"

"Maybe, maybe not," I said. "But I think I need more to go on before I try to answer anything. Let me change the question a bit: What, if anything, have you done so far about ending the affair? Maybe we can get to what you want to do by the back door."

"Well, after it was clear that Barbara was going to be all right — toward the end of the second week — Ted and I came back down here, and I told the man I was involved with about my promise. Now that I listen to myself, I suppose I was asking him to make the decision for me, just the way I was asking you a minute ago. Or maybe I thought I could actually end the affair just by telling him about the promise."

Suddenly, she looked sad. "Maybe I did, for all I know."

3

"How so? What did he say?"

"Oh, he said that as far as he was concerned, he loved me and wanted to stand by me and go on as we were. But I guess I wonder if anyone can really mean something like that after you've said you're willing to throw him away like a Kleenex when things get rough."

"You're still seeing him?"

"Yes."

"Then I guess you haven't done it yet, have you?"

"I guess not. But I still need to know if I should, don't I?"

"You have to be careful there," I said. "Let me ask you another question. You seem to have assumed that because you made a promise to God, you're bound to keep it. On what basis do you think that's true?"

She looked surprised. "On the basis that a promise to God is serious and ought to be kept. Isn't that right?"

"It depends on the kind of God you're dealing with. With most gods, that's the way the game is supposed to be played. But with the God and Father of our Lord Jesus Christ, I think not."

"You're saying that Christians don't have to keep their word to God?"

"Not exactly. I'm saying that your promises to God — or my promises or anyone else's — are not capable of getting us either accepted by God or damned by God. Acceptance, according to the Gospel, is a free gift bestowed on a world full of four-flushers. And it's given to them despite their four-flushing, right in the midst of their four-flushing. It is not a reward for hotshot behavior in the promise-keeping department. And damnation is not a punishment for breaking promises to God — or even for breaking the commandments of God himself; it's a consequence of stupidly throwing away the free gift of acceptance."

"I've heard you preach that. But where I am now, it seems either too good to be true or else just an excuse for getting away with anything you like."

4

"It always seems both," I said; "but let me keep at it anyway. Did you see the segments about Caligula in *I, Claudius* on *Masterpiece Theater?*"

"Yes. Maybe not all of them, though."

"Well, you remember Caligula. A really nasty piece of work: arrogant, cruel, and very busy working himself up to being a god while he's still alive. Anyway, when Caligula is supposedly sick to death, one of the senators makes an extravagant vow to the gods: 'My life for Caesar's if he is spared,' he says. Caligula of course gets better; and when he meets the senator after his recovery, he first expresses admiration for the vow; but then he says, 'Isn't there something wrong with this situation, though? If you offered your life for mine, we shouldn't both be here, should we?' And he sends the senator off under guard to make sure he makes good on his vow by opening a vein. Think about that a little. You made a vow to finish off your lover if your daughter was spared, and now you want to know if you have to deliver on the promise. I said the answer depended on what kind of god you made the vow to. There's no question, of course, that if you believed in a Roman-style god or in almost any god other than the Father of our Lord Jesus Christ — all of them rather nasty pieces of work, just like Caligula — the answer would be 'Yes, deliver or be damned.' But is that the kind of God you believe in?"

"I'd like to say No. But isn't the Bible full of just that sort of thing?"

"Not full by a long shot — not even in the Old Testament. There's some of it, of course. Jephthah in the Book of Judges makes a vow that if he's victorious, he'll sacrifice the first thing that comes out of his house to meet him when he comes home in triumph. Well, the first thing turns out to be his daughter; and eventually, he makes good on the vow — to her not inconsiderable regret, I should think. But you can't just pick things like that out of the Bible and decide that as they stand where you found them, they're the last word. Scripture is a revelation that takes place over time:

5

quite a few things were revealed only to be superseded by what comes later. If you were to read only the first three-fourths of the Noah story, for example, you'd decide that God's prescription for sin is destruction. But if you read the ending — which is the scriptural point of the story — it turns out that mercy, symbolized by the covenant of the rainbow, is God's real last word on sin: he says he's never going to do the destruction bit again.

"Which, of course, is exactly the case when you get to Jesus. 'The law was given through Moses; grace and truth came through Jesus Christ.' The New Testament says that God doesn't count our trespasses, that he has taken away the handwriting that was against us and nailed it to the cross. Not keeping a promise is just one more trespass he's already got tacked up there. You might, of course, make all kinds of trouble for yourself — and others as well, maybe — by breaking your vow; but then you might also make just as much trouble by keeping it. The ultimate New Testament point, however, is that whether you keep it or break it, God isn't going to count your action one way or the other: it's not going to make you any trouble with God. 'While we were still sinners, Christ died for the ungodly.' We are accepted in the Beloved, because of Jesus only, not because of anything we do."

She frowned. "I guess I know all that. But it's hard to believe."

"Correction," I said. "Nobody *knows* all that. Not you, not me, not anybody. And nobody can *feel* all that, either. Our knowledge and our feelings are all on the side of the nasty old bookkeeping gods — the divine little CPA's, the ones we think are the really respectable gods — the ones who know how to keep everybody honest, or else. But the God we believe in is not a bookkeeper, and he's not respectable. As a matter of fact, he's a crook, and he dies as one to prove it. Which is exactly why he's Good News for badly bent types like you and me. Do you see what that means? It means that if he's as weird as the Gospel says he is, we'd be well advised to stop trying to draw some neat little intellectual or emotional bead on what we think he's like, and just shut up and

6

believe in him — trust him — as he actually reveals himself in Jesus. Luther said, 'No man can know or feel he is saved; he can only *believe* it.' And believing — trusting — is simply something you *decide* to do. It's not something you can con yourself into with arguments; it's a blind 'yes' to somebody who offers you a fabulous deal for reasons you can't know anything about. But since trusting is the only way to get out of the bad news of the gods into the Good News of God in Christ, it's not as hard as you make it sound. As a matter of fact, once you get the hang of it, it's a lark."

She balked at that. "But isn't that too easy? Isn't that what they call 'cheap grace'? I mean, think about it. I come in here telling you I'm committing adultery and you practically tell me it doesn't matter. Wouldn't most priests just tell me — however gently — to cut it out?"

"Maybe. But unfortunately — or fortunately — you've got only one priest here with you now. And besides, that's not what we're talking about. Your question to me was not about adultery but about the keeping of a vow to offer up your lover for your daughter's life. What you do about adultery is up to you. Which is why my first question was 'What do *you* want to do about it?' — a question, if I recall, you didn't answer."

"I guess I was hoping you would answer the adultery question as well."

"But I didn't. And for a very simple, Gospel reason. Because if we believe the Gospel, adultery can't condemn us — and just as important, not committing adultery can't save us. What saves us is the free forgiveness of Jesus, not our works — not even our good works."

"But that's no help with the decision. I'm asking you for help because I don't know what to do. Aren't you at least supposed to tell me that adultery is wrong?"

"Why? You already know that. And if I said it to you, you would *still* have to decide what you wanted to do about it. I mean, look. The human mind is a fearful and wonderful thing. If you

7

wanted to end the adultery, you could take my condemnation of it as an endorsement of whatever emotional or relational havoc you might wreak by ending the affair. And if you didn't want to end it, you could talk yourself into deciding that while adultery in general is wrong, this particular case is something other than adultery. Either way we would still be back at what *you wanted to do*. That really is the first question. And all I will ever have to say about your answer to it is that no matter what you do, Jesus isn't going to pick up his skirts and walk around you.

"Think about the Good Samaritan for a minute. Everybody thinks they're supposed to avoid being like the priest and the Levite — the bad guys — and try to be like the Samaritan. But that misses the point. The character in the parable who most likely stands for us is the poor, beat-up guy on the ground — the guy who was such a mess he couldn't try to do anything. And what the presence of *that* character in the parable says is that no matter what you decide, or even if you never decide, Jesus doesn't give up on you. Therefore you trust *him*, and not your own efforts to save yourself."

She thought for a while. "Well, I *think* I understand: you're saying I have to answer two separate questions, right? The first is about the vow — which maybe I can see now was just stress, or something, but which turns out to be a bargain with the wrong kind of god. And the second, which I admit I really haven't asked you, and which you've refused to answer, is whether it's wrong for me to continue the affair. About that, you seem to be saying that whatever I do, Jesus won't be against me. Is that a fair summary?"

"Fair enough. But let me try to add a couple of points. First, I think you should forget about the stress factor in your vow. If the vow was a good idea, the stressful circumstances under which you made it wouldn't matter a hill of beans. The reasons why we do things are only part — sometimes even a negligible part — of the whole picture. It's possible, for example, to marry the right person, or take the right job, for crazy reasons — just as it's possible to make whopping mistakes for reasons which at the time seem totally wonderful. You have to look at what you actually *did* in order to make a sound judgment. And in this case, no matter how calm, cool, and collected you might have been when you made your vow, the Gospel fact remains that vows of that sort are not a hot idea. First of all, Jesus warns us against taking oaths like that. 'Don't swear at all,' he says; 'not by God, not by heaven, not even by earth. Let your yes be yes and your no be no.' In other words, keep your relationship with him simple. You're not dealing with a god who needs to be shaken awake by heroic measures before he'll pay attention to your interests. You're dealing with the Lord God of Elijah, not with some Baal who wants you to jump up and down all day cutting yourself with swords and lances. You're dealing with somebody who's totally on your side already and with whom you don't have to *negotiate* a thing. He's gone and negotiated the whole deal all by himself in Jesus. For Christians, the religion shop is closed. If even the Law of God can't be an instrument of salvation, your own home-brewed laws certainly can't be.

"Furthermore, Jesus teaches us to pray not to be led into temptation: 'Lead us not into a time of trial,' the Lord's Prayer says: 'Don't bring us to the test.' Now if we can be so bold as to ask God not to impose his own tests on us, we ought to be especially careful not to slap tests of our own devising on ourselves. In Jesus' death and resurrection, the whole test-passing, brownie-point-earning rigmarole of the human race has been canceled for lack of interest on God's part. All he needs from us is a simple Yes or No, and off to work he goes. If we say Yes to something wrong, or No to something right, he will reconcile it all by himself. Not only *can* he handle it, he's *already* handled it: he has all our messes fixed in Jesus — right now, even before we make them. All we have to do is trust his assurance that losers are his cup of tea. In fact, it's precisely our attempts to be winners that he warns us about: 'He who saves his life will lose it; he who loses his life for my sake and the Gospel's will save it.'

"The Reformers, you know, were very big on this. They called all such things as vows 'works of supererogation'; and they said that such things couldn't be taught without arrogancy and impiety. They insisted that no one needs to do more than plain old bounden duty. And even when you've done that, they said, you're still supposed to make no account of it: you're supposed to say, as Jesus told you, 'We are unprofitable servants.'"

She looked straight at me. "You're on your favorite hobbyhorse again. You really do think Christianity isn't a religion, don't you?"

"Absolutely. We use the forms of religion; and we certainly agree that the job of reconciliation the world's religions were trying to do is the job that needs doing. But both the Gospels and Paul insist that religion can't do the job. The blood of bulls and goats can't take away sins; your performances on your vows have no value when it comes to getting your act together so you can con God into being on your side. Only Jesus can take away sins; and he's done it all in one shot, for everybody. Religion is always bad news. Look at yourself when you came in here this morning: Ms. Grim, with the weight of working out your own reconciliation making you round-shouldered with responsibility. And all the while you were home free."

"All right," she said; "but what about adultery? You're not going to tell me you can make good news out of that, are you?"

"Not quite," I said. "But the Good News of reconciliation and forgiveness is still the most important thing about it. There is no sin you can commit that God in Jesus hasn't forgiven already. The only way you can get yourself in permanent Dutch is to refuse forgiveness. *That's* hell. The old baloney about heaven being for good guys and hell for bad guys is dead wrong. Heaven is populated entirely by forgiven sinners, not spiritual and moral aces. And hell is populated entirely by forgiven sinners. The only difference between the two groups is that those in heaven accept the forgiveness and those in hell reject it. Which is why heaven is a party — the endless wedding reception of the Lamb and his bride — and hell is nothing but the dreariest bar in town.

10

"So no matter what else you may decide about your love affair — or have already decided, for all you or I know — the first thing to decide is to trust Jesus' word that you're forgiven."

She broke in. "But if I decided to keep on with the affair, wouldn't that be some kind of defiance . . . wouldn't *that* be unforgivable? I was raised Roman Catholic. Deliberately putting yourself into an occasion of sin was supposed to be extra sinful."

"And therefore extra forgivable. Jesus dies for all the sins of everybody — for the extra-sinful ones as well as for the small-bore ones. In church, when we sing, 'Lamb of God, you take away the sins of the world,' we don't add, 'except for repeated adultery, multiple rape, persistent child-abuse, or the systematic watering of the stock of every widow in town.' For one thing, it would ruin the music. But most of all, it would bury the Good News under a pile of scholastic logic-chopping — not to mention the fact that it would limit the reach of Christ's forgiveness to a smarmy bunch of moral overachievers."

She broke in again. "But aren't we at least supposed to *try* to do what's right?"

I smiled. "Yes. But that's a subject for another day. Right now, all I want to note is that this conversation is going in a very odd direction. I'm the priest and you're the parishioner. But for some reason — probably your early R.C. experience — you've decided to play the priest. I'm trying to sell you absolutely free grace and Good News; but you keep coming back at me as if you were old Father Paschal O'Toole in the confessional box on a Saturday night. So I'm just going to change the subject — or, to be accurate, get back to the subject I've been trying to get us onto all along — namely, what *you* actually want to do about the affair.

"As I see it, there are four possibilities. One, you really haven't decided what you want. Two, you've already decided — one way or the other — but you want me to help you face your decision. Three, your lover has by now decided on his own to call it off and you want help with that. And four, you will never decide. (That fourth possibility, of course, is just for the sake of symmetry. In actual fact, the first three cover the whole waterfront of meaningful options; even if you never decided what you wanted to do about the affair, you would still have to decide what you wanted to do about such an indecisive, drifting life.)"

She started to say something, but I held up a finger to stop her.

"Let me keep going, okay? Otherwise I'll lose count. Think about possibility number one: you haven't yet decided what you want. All I have to say about that is that unless you choose terminal drift, you *will* decide by and by, and I'll be here to help you through whatever it is you decide. Seriously. We can go through as much of this as you want as often as you need to go through it. But since I don't figure you as the drifting type, I think it won't be too long before you land on one side or the other.

"Which brings us to number two — the possibility that you've already decided. You talk as if you want to call it off; but you mentioned that you've been in contact with your lover since you came back from Vermont. How many times on the phone and how many times in person? Roughly."

She looked right at me. "Five times altogether in person and I don't know how many times on the phone."

"I think you should think about that. It has at least the ring of a positive decision about it. And if it is that, you have some more decisions to make — or at least some more clarification to achieve about what you really want to do. I don't know much about your marriage, and I don't want you to try and tell me about it today. But there are at least a couple of possibilities there. You could want out of your marriage. If that's so, and if you acted on it, you would have a whole string of new decisions to make — and, of course, a whole new life to enjoy, or cope with, or suffer from, as the case might be. On the other hand, you could want just a long-standing affair; and if that were so, you'd have most of the above problems and/or opportunities, plus the need for rather

12

large amounts of prudence, restraint, stamina, luck, and the ability to keep two sets of wires permanently uncrossed. You can tell me next time about all that, too. Meanwhile, since I have to go and make some hospital calls in a few minutes, let me head for the barn with the last possibility — namely, that your lover will decide to end the affair on his own.

"Right now, that sounds less than likely to me, but I could be wrong. In any case, we'll see. Even if he does, though, what *you* want is not necessarily irrelevant. For one thing, you could kick and scream against ending it: given the vicissitudes of the human will, you might just turn him around. But then again you might not. And in that case you'd have been dumped — maybe even, as you suggested, dumped through your own fault. But even in that case, I'll be here if you need me. For what it's worth, I've been dumped myself — very much through my own fault — and it was definitely not a lot of fun. (I've also done my share of dumping, and that was no barrel of monkeys, either.) So whichever way you go, I know a little about the territory. Next time, okay? Call me when and if you're ready to talk some more."

She stood up. "Any parting words of wisdom?"

"Yes. Make your communion every Sunday come hell or high water, and say the Lord's Prayer every day."

I got up, walked over to her, and made the sign of the cross on her forehead: "The Lord Almighty bless you, the Father, the Son, and the Holy Spirit. Amen. See you around, Helen."

TWO

The Mystery and Guilt

N ow then. Time to give you the reader a bit more of a clue
as to what I'm doing.

The subject of this book is *the Mystery of Christ*. In the Bible,
this concept is referred to not only as the mystery of Christ, but
also as *the mystery of God* (or of *God's will*), *the mystery of the
kingdom,* and *the mystery of the gospel*. In all cases, though, it refers
to something *hidden* (*my-* is the root of the Greek verb *myein:* "to
be shut," or "closed"). At the risk of leaving you more mystified
than you would like to be, however, I shall add only one comment
here: whatever else this Mystery of Christ may be, it is something
hidden *in this world* — in the physical universe. It is not some
"mystical" truth parked way off in "heaven" or in some other realm
of "spiritual reality." But since we have a whole book's worth of
time in which to talk about this topic, let me move on to the
subject of how I propose to deal with it.

I've already given you one counseling session, and I intend
to give you more. All of them are based on conversations I have
had with real persons; but all of them have been fictionalized —
in two ways. For one thing, I have changed names and place
references (and even sexes, sometimes) in order to protect the
confidentiality of the original exchanges. Not only that, but I have

14

occasionally combined situations involving two different people and presented them as a single case.

For a second and more important thing, though, even when my accounts feature only one person, they are not verbatim records of what transpired on the original occasion. I keep no such records, and I have a notoriously bad memory for the literal details of my conversations with others. Accordingly, a great deal of what you will be reading has been made up in the process of my writing it. When the author of a novel composes dialogue, she or he does not work from a set of index cards containing the *ipsissima verba* of the characters. Instead, the author writes down a remark or portrays an action consistent with character number one and then, shifting to the mind-set of character number two, formulates a reply or a reaction that will be consistent with that second point of view. If an author, therefore, writes twenty pages of dialogue, or twenty chapters, she may well end up very far removed indeed from what she had originally thought her characters would say, or even from where she first imagined they would finally arrive. Authors explain this peculiarity by saying that fictional characters "have minds of their own"; and they refuse to let themselves as creators straitjacket the freedom of their creatures. All I am saying here is that the same thing has happened to me in writing up these "cases": a good deal of what I and my opposite number in these dialogues say was never said on land or sea before it was said here. It is, however, quite consistent with what the "counselee," as I understand him or her, would say; and it is (I think) totally consistent with what I myself would say, given the circumstances portrayed.

But enough demurrers. The sessions I shall portray for you will cover a range of problems and puzzlements people have laid before me as a priest of the Episcopal Church — or, to widen the reference a bit, as a member of the clergy available to everyone and his sister for pastoral counseling. In addition to Helen, whom you just read about, there will be five other persons (two more women and three men) who find themselves in conversation with me disclosing their personal, if unrecognized, encounters with the Mystery of Christ.

In depicting these counseling sessions, I have set myself a strict rule: the chapters in which they are presented will consist entirely of dialogue; they will contain not a single comment or surmise about what was going on in the unexpressed thoughts of either party. I will not second-guess what my conversational partner was thinking; and I will scrupulously avoid even hinting at what I myself knew or thought at the time. In these chapters I want you as the reader to be simply a fly on the wall — listening and watching, but not having to deal with anybody's conclusions but your own about what's going on.

In the chapter following each of the sessions, however, you and I will sit down and have at each other. You, perhaps, may object violently to something I said, or even to everything I said. I, on the other hand, may feel that you misread me, or that you read me correctly and are dead wrong in objecting. I shall, of course, have to do a little authorial guesswork as to your thoughts. But that will be part of the fun: if I guess well, you may be moved to trust my other fictions; if badly, perhaps what I have to say will apply to some other reader but still be interesting to you. In any case, these even-numbered chapters will be yours and mine: yours (with luck) to hear your concerns addressed; and mine to defend or confirm my counsel and to inch this book forward toward an understanding of the Mystery of Christ.

Why this roundabout approach? Well, to begin with, because it's more entertaining than trying to dump straight academic theology in your lap. But there is another reason, one that comes out of my personal convictions about how pastoral counseling (that is, *counseling by ordained Christian pastors*) ought to be done. I see pastoral counseling, at its root, as a straightforward extension of my commission to proclaim the Gospel and administer the sacraments of the church. *As a pastor,* therefore, my real authority —

my true authenticity, whether in the pulpit, or in my office, or in the confessional, or at the end of a piano at a cocktail party — lies in my fidelity to the Gospel, not in my assorted competences (real or imagined) in other fields.

Let me explain what I mean. I have (I think) some real competences. I am a professional theologian of at least some standing. I am also an accomplished cook, food writer, and teacher of cooking. I have a good grasp of the politics of human relationships. And I am a decent woodworker, a fair musician, and a diligent runner of the roads. On the other hand, I am neither a psychiatrist nor a psychologist; I am not a trained hospital chaplain; and I am not well-versed in such things as family systems therapy or twelve-step programs. Other clergy you might come across will have other lists of competences. They might even be professionals in all the fields about which I know next to nothing; but, on the other hand, they might not be able to theologize (or cook) their way through a cobweb.

I note all this because there is a tendency now to suppose that the way to train clergy to be good pastoral counselors is to give them professional competence in what are usually called the "helping professions" — to make them trained psychologists, or knowledgeable hospital visitors, or family-systems adepts, or twelve-step experts. I have no objection to such professionalization in and of itself: competence in any department is not to be sneezed at. But I do think that in the rush to become professionals in fields that unordained persons are perfectly capable of handling, the clergy can lose sight of their principal competence as counselors — of their calling to be authentic and authoritative proclaimers of the Gospel, the Good News of God in Christ.

There was a time, of course, back in the days when theology was thought of as "the queen of the sciences," when a correspondingly false conclusion was drawn about pastoral counseling: the pastor's job, it was then assumed, was to give troubled people correct instruction in theology — most often, in moral theology.

If someone came to a priest contemplating suicide, for example, the presumption was that the priest's job was to tell him suicide was wrong because it was the one sin he would have no time to repent of — and which would, accordingly, be unforgivable. Likewise, if someone came contemplating an abortion, or a lie, or (like Helen, perhaps) the continuance of an adulterous relationship, the pastor's principal job was supposed to be getting her back on the theologically correct track so she could become a non-sinner. But that approach has a number of very large booby-traps in it. One is that it buries the Gospel: Jesus didn't say he came to judge sinners, or even to turn them into non-sinners; he said he came to *save* them. And the rest of the New Testament makes it quite clear that his salvation works by *grace through faith*, not by frightening people into getting their act together. A second booby-trap of the approach is that it puts all the people who don't, can't, or won't get their act together (and that includes all of us, in one department or another) outside the reach of God's forgiveness in Christ — a forgiveness, presumably, offered to the whole world, sin notwithstanding: "While we were *still sinners,* Christ died for the ungodly."

But the third booby-trap is potentially the most Gospel-obscuring one of all. Theology — whether dogmatic, or moral, or ascetic, or whatever — is fundamentally *systematic thought about what you believe.* Therefore, *it is only as good as the system you invent to do your thinking with.* Let me illustrate. The supposedly correct advice for the potential suicide in the previous paragraph depends on two assumptions: one, that repentance after suicide is impossible; and two, that nonrepentance prevents God from forgiving people. But those assumptions are not based on the Gospel. They are based in the first instance on a philosophical conclusion (a human soul that has lost its body has no way of *doing anything*), and in the second instance on a view of God that contradicts some of Jesus' major parables (the parable of the Prodigal Son, to name only one, in which the father forgives the prodigal *before* he makes

18

his confession — Luke 15:11-32). Accordingly, it seems to me that when pastoral advice is given by an ordained person, it ought to be given primarily on the basis of what he or she was ordained to do — namely, witness to the Good News of God in Christ — and not on the basis of any other competence (or incompetence) the pastor in question may possess.

True enough, the competences of individual pastors will always be a prominent feature of their counseling. I, for example, toss around a fair amount of theology when I advise people. But not because it's theology they need to hear from me (even if they think they do) — only because theology is *my subject,* and I habitually think in its terms. Another pastor might well be a board-certified psychiatrist; she would just as naturally think and counsel in psychiatric terms. But, once again, it is her authenticity as an ordained witness to the Good News, not as a psychiatrist, that should be the deepest root of her pastoral counseling.

Let me tie up all these observations about the role conferred by ordination with one further comment. Ordained persons are not commissioned to do certain things for the church that the rest of the church cannot or does not do. Rather, they are ordained as *sacraments,* as *signs to the church* of what the whole church is commissioned to do — namely, bear the apostolic witness to Jesus' death and resurrection. When I go into the pulpit on Easter Day, for example, I do not go as an expert on the scientific or theological possibilities of resurrection. If I do my job correctly, I do not stand up there and tell the congregation that I have studied the subject and have come to this, that, or the other conclusion about it. Instead, I arrive in the pulpit as the latest in a long line of runners, and I tell them very simply, but very authoritatively, "Peter saw him risen . . . (pant, pant, pant) . . . and he told me to tell you." Do you see? When I preach the Good News, I am first of all an apostle, not a theologian or any other kind of learned person. And accordingly, when I counsel, I consider myself first and foremost an apostle and not anything else. That and that alone is the taproot of my pastoral authenticity as a preacher, or a counselor, or a confessor, or even as a husband, father, or friend. That and that alone is why I have been ordained.

❦   ❦

But enough of that for now. You and I need to talk.

Perhaps your first difficulty with what I said to Helen is the same as hers. Why, you want to ask me, was I so resistant to telling her that her adultery was wrong and should be broken off? Why was my first really challenging question to her, What did *she* want to do about it? And why, above all, did I keep returning to that question again and again? (Helen, incidentally, may be back later in this book. So, leaving further developments in her situation till then, I shall confine my answers strictly to what was going on in my mind during the session you already witnessed.)

It seemed to me that Helen, like many people who come for advice, came in a state that she would have described as confusion, but that would more accurately be described as fear. She was afraid of doing, or not doing, something that would get her in Dutch — principally in Dutch with God, but also, to a lesser and less clearly perceived extent, with others in her life. About those fears, I had only two things I wanted to say. As far as her fear of making trouble for the others in her life was concerned, there was no way of my getting rid of her fear. She had already embarked on the affair; no matter what she chose to do, she was bound to hurt somebody. If she broke it off, she would probably treat her lover (and herself) badly; if she kept it going, she might well treat her husband badly; and if she divorced her husband and married her lover, that could be at least as large a can of worms as anything else. There simply was no course open to her that would be non-fearful. Therefore, there was no way I or anyone else could take away her fears by giving her specific advice to go one way or another. She wanted "Daddy" to make it all better, of course; but given the rules of the game she had put herself in, the only thing Daddy could do was suggest that she have the courage to do whatever she did with both hands, and then offer her a shoulder to cry on, however it worked out.

That, incidentally, is an instance of pastoral counseling at almost its lowest level. You don't have to be an ordained witness to the resurrection to give that kind of advice; you just have to be a realist. But since at all the upper levels of genuinely pastoral counseling you will be dealing with people who would dearly love to have reality suspended in their case, it helps mightily if you give them a dose of realism early on. Because if the Gospel is about anything, it is about a God who meets us where we are, not where we ought to be — "while we were still sinners," as Paul said, and as I keep insisting. And therefore, if you are eventually going to reassure someone that she doesn't have to fear coming to a God whose cup of tea is real situations, however messy, it's not a bad idea to disabuse her of the notion that her situation must somehow be made unmessy before she can qualify for God's attention. Such counsel, accordingly, comes under the heading of what they used to call a *praeparatio evangelica,* a preparation for the Gospel. It isn't exactly good news as such; but it's good enough for openers because the true Good News is that God works in bad news. (See the Lost Sheep, the Prodigal Son, and the rest of Jesus' parables about messy situations . . . right on up to the crucifixion, which is the last word in messes.)

Which brings me to the second thing I wanted to say. Helen's principal fear was that God would be mad at her if she broke her promise, or continued in the adultery, or whatever. *That* fear I think I did address with genuine, top-level pastoral counseling. I authoritatively told her that wherever she got that idea about God, it wasn't from Jesus or the New Testament, or even from the Bible as a whole (if you read it fairly as the sometimes difficult but always progressive revelation it actually is). Her god, I told her, is not the God and Father of our Lord Jesus Christ whom I was commis-

21

sioned to represent — and whom she, as a Christian, supposedly trusts. She spent a good bit of time, of course, trying to ace me into admitting that her god was the true one, and that mine was the product of an aberrant and excessively easygoing state of mind. But I never gave her an inch. And I refused to do so because I'm convinced that while people are indeed able to hear the Good News — and hear it gladly because it's obviously the sweetest deal they're ever going to be offered — they can't listen to it for long without pulling the wet blanket of their fear-mongering theology back down over their heads. They're actually more rattled by the liberating, guilt-abolishing news of grace than they are by their fears.

Speaking of fear, I want to go back for a moment to the word "Daddy" I introduced a few paragraphs earlier. In spite of the fact that people have an inveterate hankering to put the church *in loco parentis* — and in spite of the fact that the church, more often than not, has gleefully thrown itself into the role of being everybody's Mommy and Daddy — the whole exercise is a terrible idea. This insidious, parental image of the church doesn't conform to what even a halfway decent parent actually does. Only rotten fathers and mothers ride roughshod over their children's freedom to make mistakes. Only the worst parents ever suggest that there are unforgivable acts that will, unless avoided by the children, be the death of parental love. Only the most dreadful grown-ups use fear to control the young. That there are a good number of such disreputable types (and that all of us, to some degree, are equally disreputable) should not blind us to the fact that the concept of God as an angry, unforgiving parent — and of his church as a domineering grown-up issuing threats to willful kids — is bad news, not Gospel. Such concepts inculcate only fear: fear of God, and then fear of our own freedom. They lead not to the liberty of the children of God, to the freedom with which Christ has set us free, but to a servile mentality that kills courage and breeds resentment. Still, much of the church, clergy and laity alike, goes blithely on perpetuating its parental image. And then we have the nerve to wonder why so many people hate themselves for being sheep, and hate the church for making them such.

That is why the church needs perpetually to recover its grip on the Gospel, the Good News of grace and forgiveness, and to protest in every age against theological models that blow the Gospel out of the water. Indeed, that is the reason I am writing this book: to protest against just such a model (a model I choose to call *transactionalism*), and to witness to a better model based on *the Mystery of Christ.* Because while it is indeed quite sufficient for all purposes, here or hereafter, to say you *trust* Jesus as your savior — to affirm, as the ultimate concern in your life, a relationship of faith with him as a person — almost nobody is able to let it go at that. You almost always proceed directly to *think* about what you believe in; and that thinking inevitably ends up producing *theological models* of various kinds, some of which are more hazardous to the Gospel than others.

Accordingly, let me illustrate the dangers of theologizing with two models: a bad one, based on *transactional* imagery, and a good one, based on *the Mystery of Christ.*

In both models, you start with the same fundamental thought developed out of your act of faith in Jesus and your reading of the basic assertions of the New Testament — namely, that God takes away the sins of the world in the death and resurrection of Jesus. So far, so good.

But then, if you keep on thinking, you will inevitably come up with some questions: *How* does the death and resurrection of Jesus (an event that, on the face of the biblical narrative, happened some two thousand years ago) make itself operative in your life here and now on the brink of the twenty-first century? How indeed is it operative for anyone in any age? What you have handed yourself by raising these questions, you see, is the job of constructing a *theological model* of the way the divine operation works.

The kind of model you build from this point on, however,

will depend very much on your answers to some prior questions — questions you may very well have answered already by going along with certain assumptions based on a transactional model you have never consciously criticized. You may have assumed, for example, that because the gift of grace in Jesus' death and resurrection is something you receive by faith, this gift is something you do not have *until* you make the act of faith. In other words, you may have assumed that the gift starts out by being in *one person* (namely, Jesus) *and not in anybody else,* and that it enters the lives of other persons *only after the completion of some suitable transaction* on their part. And this assumption, if you continue to hold it, will lead you down the garden path to a theology that is clean contrary to some of the most fundamental points in the New Testament.

Because despite the fact that both the Epistle to the Romans and the Epistle to the Galatians make it quite clear that the gift of grace operates by faith alone and not by works, you have for all practical purposes converted faith into a species of work. You have turned it into something that needs to be *done* before the gift can in fact be bestowed. And that in turn leads you into frank opposition to all the assertions in Jesus' parables and in Paul's writings — and in the formularies of the church, for that matter — that clearly say the gift is given *without any conditions at all.* You have said, in short, that it must be *earned.* But Jesus says (e.g., in the parable of the Laborers in the Vineyard — Matt. 20:1-16) that the reward has nothing to do with merit. And Paul says (e.g., in Rom. 3–5) that a person is justified *"without works"* and that "while we were *still sinners,* Christ died for the *ungodly."* And the Nicene Creed that says we acknowledge *"one baptism"* — not a bunch of subsequent transactions — "for the forgiveness of sins."

But in building this theological model you have also done something else. You have opened yourself to the idea that the church is the fellowship of those who have the gift and that the rest of the world is just a crowd of outcasts who don't have it. Even though you may go on saying in church that the Lamb of God takes away the sins of the world, you are actually holding that he has taken away only the sins of the church. And from there, you are in danger of waltzing yourself into the position that the world at large is damned unless it joins the church, and that even the children of Christians will go to hell if they are not baptized — and so on and on, right into the theological house of horrors that all too many people actually think is the household of faith.

So if you are wise, you will go back to the drawing board as promptly as possible and try to design a theological model that does less damage. Needless to say, the model I think you should try to construct will not be based on transactions like earning, working, deserving, or any other tit-for-tat operation. Rather, it will be based on the imagery of what you say you really believe in anyway — namely, the imagery of a free gift *already given, without condition, to everybody* — a gift *hidden* in every particle of creation, a gift that goes by the name of *the Mystery of Christ.*

For the record, the phrase "the mystery of Christ" appears only in the Epistles to the Ephesians and to the Colossians; but the notion of the work of God in the world as a "mystery" — as a reconciling gift hidden throughout creation — appears more widely. It can be found in the Gospels (e.g., in Jesus' parable of the Yeast Hidden in the Dough — Matt. 13:33, or in the parable of the Treasure Hidden in a Field — Matt. 13:44); but it also occurs in Romans and 1 Corinthians. This Mystery, as the New Testament presents it, is not at all a transaction poked into a universe that previously didn't have the benefit of it. Rather, it is a *cosmic dispensation* that has been present at all times and in all places but "kept secret for ages and generations" (Rom. 16:25). It is a dispensation, in fact, that has been hidden "from the foundation of the world" (Matt. 13:35), or even "before the foundation of the world" (Eph. 1:4) until it could finally be revealed in Jesus. In other words, the mysterious, reconciling grace that was revealed in Jesus is not something that got its act in gear for the first time in Jesus; rather, it is a feature of the very constitution of the universe

— a feature that was there all along, for everybody and everything. And it was there, Christians believe, because the Person who manifests himself finally and fully in Jesus' humanity is none other than the Word of God, the Second Person of the Three Persons in One God who is intimately and immediately present to every scrap of creation from start to finish.

By way of an apology for that outburst of scriptural quotation and theological jargon, let me give you an illustration.

Suppose I were to tell you that I had already buried, under a flat rock on a piece of property you own, $1,000,000 in crisp, new $1,000 bills. And suppose I were also to tell you that I have no intention of ever taking this money back: it's there, and that's that. On one level, I have given you a piece of sensationally good news: you are the possessor of a million bucks, no conditions attached, no danger of my reneging on the gift. And if you trust me — that is, if you go to your property and start turning over flat rocks — you will sooner or later actually be able to relate to the million I so kindly gave you. But note something crucial. Your faith (your trust) does not earn you the money, nor does it con me into giving it to you: the money was yours all along just because I was crazy enough to bury it in your backyard. Your faith, you see, is in no way the *cause* of the gift; the only thing it can possibly have any causal connection with is *your own enjoyment of the gift.*

So much for your *faith* in my mysterious, hidden gift. But suppose now that instead of running out and lifting rocks, you sat down and started *thinking* about my gift — started, as it were, to *theologize* about it. At that point the million dollars could easily cease to be good news and become nothing but a problem. You might, for example, decide that I was talking through my hat, or that I had a perverse desire to wear you out hoisting stones, or that no one in his right mind would actually do what I claimed, or that you didn't deserve such a gift, or that it was impossible for me to give such a gift, or even (if I gave you the good news of the gift through a representative and not in person) that I didn't exist.

In any case, the longer you thought such thoughts, the less likely you would be to bother turning over rocks.

But perhaps you see the point sufficiently at least to allow me to get back to Helen. It was the model of the million dollars under the rock that lay behind my initial counseling of her. And it was her model of the gift as something to be earned or bargained for that I was trying to get her to drop. As I said, we may see by and by what she decides about her love affair. But the reason why, in that first session, I refused to nudge her even mildly in the direction of a decision was that I saw no point in encouraging her to do anything for some deity who definitely is not the God and Father of our Lord Jesus Christ. In particular, my point in speaking to her as I did was to get her off the subject of guilt — or, better said, to disabuse her of her conviction that she could be acceptable to God only if she could manage to render herself not guilty. And I did that because guilt, as we commonly conceive it, is neither a New Testament nor even a Christian category. We see guilt as something that will condemn us unless we can get rid of it. Gospel Christianity sees it as something God has gotten rid of for us, free for nothing. "There is therefore now *no condemnation* for those who are in Christ Jesus," says Paul (Rom. 8:1): God has declared a blanket *presumption of innocence* over every one of us — a presumption based on the fact that he has gone ahead and made us innocent already in his Beloved Son.

And therefore, since the gracious work of Christ Jesus is already in everybody and for everybody simply because he's the God who holds everything in his loving, forgiving hands, the root premise of my counsel to Helen was just this: *the guilt shop has been closed*, boarded up entirely and for good by God's grace and nothing else. All she needs to do is trust that million-dollar news and let the liberating relationship it has already established happen. *She never has to spend another penny in the guilt department.*

Oh, I know. That gives you problems. You're worried that it might give people the idea that they have permission to sin. Well, I

27

have news for you: everybody, to the best of my knowledge, already has permission to do any damned-fool thing he or she can get away with. That doesn't make it smart to sin or fun to sin, or even make sin a good idea because it gives grace a chance to abound. But it does mean that God, on the available evidence, is not seriously in the sin-prevention business. He's in the sin-forgiving business: "I judge no one," Jesus said; "I did not come to judge the world but to save the world" (John 12:47). No matter what we do, therefore, we are off the judgment hook as long as we are in this life — and we are off it forever as well, I think, because if you read the judgment passages in Scripture in the light of the irrevocable grace that the New Testament posits as the heart of God's plan, you come up with a distinctly happier picture even of the Last Judgment.

But that's a large subject, and it will certainly come up again. Since this is already a long chapter — and since I still have those hospital calls to make — let's move on.

THREE

Michael

It was a Monday morning in late June when Michael dropped in for one of his occasional talks with me. For the record, he was twenty-one, single, an accomplished graphic artist, and had completed two years' work at two different upstate colleges. Now, after a year off to "find himself," he was thinking about returning to the second college in the fall.

The peer relationships that Michael actively pursued (at any rate, the ones he talked to me about) were predominantly with males. Most of the time he was able to speak fairly easily of himself as gay, but now and then he would ask me what I thought of "the hang-ups other people have" about homosexuality. But he never spoke (nor did I ever inquire) about the physical details of his relationships. In any case, he had been in therapy more or less continuously for three years and was still seeing the local psychiatrist who perhaps knew him better than the other counselors he had seen when he was away at school.

At the first college he had attended, he had become involved with a Christian student group that leaned in the direction of fundamentalism — a position about which he had reservations even then. At the second college, he had gravitated to another group which, while still strongly evangelical, was more to his liking

29

because it contained people who, as he put it, "weren't such biblical literalists that they had to condemn everybody who disagreed with them about moral questions." He was not an Episcopalian, but he attended the Episcopal Church at least as often as any, citing its "openness to different opinions" as the reason for his preference. His conversations with me were mostly about theological questions, but they included side trips into the moral and romantic aspects of his relationships.

"What's new or different?" I asked Michael after we'd exchanged a few pleasantries and settled down.

"Not a whole lot — except I've pretty much decided to go back to school in the fall."

"Still the same place as last time around?"

"Yes. It's less of a hassle than trying to get used to a whole new situation. Besides, after a year away, I actually miss the place."

"The place, or the people?" I asked.

"Both, I guess; but mostly the people. I've kept in touch with a few of them. Anyway, I think it's time for me to get out of here. The year off seems to have come to a dead end."

"How so?"

"You remember I told you about the friend I was involved with? Jon?"

"Yes," I said. "He was working at a museum, right? Up Island somewhere. Thirtyish. Yale fine-arts type, if I remember correctly."

"That's him. I just don't feel I can go on with the relationship anymore."

"What happened?"

"I suppose I more or less knew about him all along, but I just thought he was going to be different with me."

"Different from . . . ?"

"From his pattern. For a while I thought he was as involved with me as I was with him. I mean, he was somebody I could finally talk to about anything that bothered me without having him get distant. But lately he's started talking about how I should see other people and not be so wrapped up in him. It turns out he's been seeing others all along."

"How do you know that?"

"Some of my friends told me a while ago. I sat on the information as long as I could, but finally I had to bring it up to him. He just admitted it and told me I should feel free to do the same."

Michael hesitated. I let a couple of beats go by and said, "Ah! Romance. You know what romance is like? It's like cooking. The number of people who can actually bring it off is minuscule compared with the number who claim they can. The preoccupation with it may be universal, but the talent for it is unevenly distributed. The world always contains more rotten cooks and lovers than good ones."

"That sounds cynical."

"It isn't. It's just a fact. St. Thomas Aquinas said somewhere that philosophy shouldn't be studied by youths — by which he meant anyone under fifty. He died at forty-nine, of course, so he didn't practice what he preached. But you could probably say the same thing about romance: even though everyone studies it like mad, it takes a couple of genuine grown-ups to get it right — and even in the over-fifty set, such types are hard to find. But that makes you cynical only if you let it. If you have the stomach for romance, you can survive it even if you're a nine-year-old. In fact, developing a stronger stomach is not a bad definition of growing up. In romance, you get served (and you serve) a lot of indigestible dishes — stuff that for one reason or another you (or your partner) can't stand. If you're wise, you don't let yourself get sour about that. You just put up with the indigestion, forgive the rotten cooking, and look forward to a better meal some other day."

"That's not much help in the present, though. My gut tells me I was used. And the feeling doesn't go away."

"What feeling? Hurt, or anger?"

"Both. What difference does it make?"

31

"A lot. Hurt, you have to wait out. But one way or another, as long as you don't deny it or shove it so far down it festers, it goes away. Anger, though, doesn't go away by itself. It's not enough just to avoid repressing it; you have to make a deliberate effort to get rid of it. You have to forgive."

"Even a bastard?"

"Especially a bastard. And only partly because forgiving is a nice thing to do for a person who wasn't nice. Mostly, you have to do it for yourself. Because unless you do, you're inviting the bastard to take up residence inside you indefinitely. You'll have him with you consciously for as long as you can keep up your enthusiasm for beating the dead horse of your pain. And then — after you've gotten over the hurt — you'll have him there unconsciously giving you a jaundiced view of the motives of everyone you get close to. In the name of your trigger-happy sense of justice, you'll always be expecting more of people than they're likely to deliver."

"Forgiving isn't all that easy."

"I'm not saying it is; only that it's essential. Even God forgives: he says he will *remember our sins no more* — that he'll just forget about them and won't harp on some exalted degree of justice that's not about to be forthcoming. So if the Ruler of the universe can set such a low standard for his own justice, it ill behooves the rest of us to sit around making a career out of keeping scores."

He frowned. "You keep knocking justice. You're saying it's a bad idea?"

"Not exactly. It's just that in the hands of anyone who's not willing to lay down his life for his friends — or his enemies, for that matter — the sense of justice can be a killer. And not just a killer of the person you decide is unjust but a killer of your own ability to relate to anybody. Sooner or later you'll have to bump off everyone in your life, because sooner or later you'll find they're all sinners — all unjust. Righteousness is a scarce commodity. And people who will give you everything you think you justly deserve are even scarcer than righteous ones.

32

"But look," I said. "Before I lose my thread completely, do me a favor. Remember some key words for me. I want to say something about *Anger,* then *Romance,* then *Angels,* and then maybe *Gossip.* It comes out to A, R, A, G: 'ARAG.' Got that?"

"Yes. Anger, Romance, Angels, Gossip."

"Good. You're a genius. But genius and wisdom have to be gotten into the same stadium before they can play ball. Let's go.

"Anger first. The key to understanding anger is that it always arises out of an offended sense of justice. You can't get truly angry at someone unless you can convince yourself he has willfully deprived you of something that was reasonably and rightfully due you. If a friend unwittingly backs over your old, stone-deaf dog because it was asleep under the right rear wheel of his car, you may be sad and hurt over the dog, but you can't seriously be angry at your friend. (You might, of course, work up a case for being angry at God for making a world in which such things can happen; but that's only because you went hunting for an injustice on somebody's part to provide yourself with a provable villain whose unfairness would allow you to convert your hurt into anger.) But if the guest comes tearing needlessly up your driveway at forty miles an hour and kills the dog, you don't have to hunt for the injustice in heaven: you've got it right in the driver's seat of an overpowered sports car.

"Therefore, the first thing you can do to defuse your anger at someone close to you is to take an honest look at the balance sheet of injustices between the two of you. If you do that, you'll probably find that the unjust behavior that made you angry with your friend was itself the product of his anger at you — of his sense that something he had assumed was due him from you was withheld, or that something he didn't deserve was dumped on him. You follow me?"

"Yes. But how does that get you to forgiveness?"

"Actually it doesn't. As a matter of fact, we haven't gotten anywhere near forgiveness yet. We're only at the level of trying to see that there are usually two sides to these things, and then of understanding that maybe even forgiveness is too lordly and one-sided an exercise, given the general untidiness of the situation. Maybe there are injustices on both sides, and the two of you can just bring yourselves to shut up about the whole business. That may seem like a low level on which to deal with injustice, but I think I can make a case that it isn't. For one thing, it has the same goal as forgiveness, but it doesn't have the same high price tag. The object of forgiveness is the restoration of relationship. And the device by which it works is the death and resurrection of the forgiver — his dropping dead to his own right to justice so that at least he himself can rise to the possibility of a restored relationship. If he doesn't do that, his only alternative is to kill his unjust former friend and, as a result, the relationship. But if you can manage to say, 'I'm as wrong in my way as he is in his,' then maybe you can call a truce instead of having to declare World War III.

"For a second thing, though, the image of the divine forgetting I quoted you a while ago (from Jeremiah 31:34, about the final covenant of mercy) suggests that even God is not above dropping the subject of sins. If you think about the death of God incarnate in Jesus on the cross, what is that if not the gift of God's silence to the world? After millennia of divine jawboning about the holiness of justice and the wickedness of sin, God himself simply shuts up about the whole business. He dies as a criminal, under the curse of the Law — as if to say, 'Look, I'm as guilty as you are in this situation because I set it up in the first place; let's just forget about blame and get on with the party.' "

Michael broke in quickly. "But what did I do to Jon that was in any way like what he did to me?"

"Obviously, I don't know enough to say," I told him. "But maybe you do. Think about it. Maybe there was something he expected as justice in your relationship — something due him from you that he couldn't stand not getting. It doesn't have to be a correct or even a fair expectation in actual fact; all that matters is

34

that he had it, and that your not giving him what he thought he deserved entitled him to be angry — or at least sufficiently pissed off with your behavior to want you out of his hair. Did he ever complain about you, or about subjects you brought up? Were there ever situations between you in which he seemed to back away from you, to push you off to a distance where you'd be less disturbing or threatening to him?"

Michael thought about that for a while. "Well, he didn't like to hear me talk about the doubts I sometimes still have about my gay life-style — or about religious or moral questions, either, now that I think of it."

"Can you think of anything that might help you understand *why* he didn't like those conversations?"

Michael started to say something but then stopped.

"Keep going, if you can," I said. "Maybe you'll get somewhere."

"Oh, I was just thinking of a word he used all the time in those conversations. He called them 'heavy.' And as often as not, he ended up telling me *I* was heavy."

"Were you, do you think?"

He clamped his lips together and gave a little shrug. "I guess I can be at times. Other people have told me that too. But friends don't always have to be light, do they? Doesn't real friendship mean being able to share everything?"

"Yes," I said. "But real friends are as hard to find as good cooks. Did you ever see the old ads for Father Flanagan's Boys' Town? They had a picture of one little kid carrying another on his back; the caption was 'Shucks, Father, he ain't heavy, he's my brother.' Well, some wit took the picture and gave it a new caption: 'Shucks, Father, he ain't my brother, he's heavy.' You think maybe there's something buried way down in Jon that makes him prefer the second caption to the first?"

"Maybe. I've often thought that his charm is partly an effort to keep everybody light and therefore at a safe distance. He just never lets up on it. It's almost as if he's *rigidly* charming — as if he doesn't *dare* let anyone get too close."

"Well . . . that's something to think about, you know. Maybe he had a whole childhood of being dumped on, and the charm was a frantic effort to control the dumpers by keeping them happy, happy, happy."

"I also thought of something else," Michael said. "Jon always acts as if he has absolutely no problems with being gay. He's almost aggressively confident about it. Charming, but aggressive. I've wondered sometimes whether that isn't a cover for some doubts he doesn't want to face. It would certainly explain why he didn't want me bringing up doubts."

"That it would. It wouldn't necessarily mean that his doubts, or his apprehensions, or his feelings of being spooked by his own gayness were the same as yours. But since no one can break with the societal norms he's been raised with without feeling a little spooky sometimes, the spookiness is not something he'd enjoy having to face just because somebody else wanted to bring it up.

"In any case," I added, "that's two things for you to think about in the understanding department. Plus one more. Just as there are some really terrific cooks scattered around in the great dismal kitchen of the world, there are some really terrific friends out there if you're willing to take a few lumps looking for them. Maybe Jon did you a favor. Maybe you owe him more thanks than anger. Maybe seeing his back will be a bigger treat than his front ever was. But enough about anger. What's next?"

Michael smiled and said, "ARAG: Romance."

"Excellent. I might even have remembered it myself, especially since we've just about gotten to it, anyway. Tell me something. Would it be fair for me to assume that you are, or at least were, in love with Jon?"

He nodded.

"Okay. So let me talk about why we fall in love with the particular, if not peculiar, people we do — why it's just with them, and not with every character who comes along, that the contraption of Romance gets itself into gear. Some of what I have to say is lifted cold out of a book called *Getting the Love You Want* (a God-awful title, by the way, which I'll bet was slapped on by the publisher because it sounded self-helpy). The author, incidentally, is a preacher-turned-professional-counselor named Harville Hendrix; but since a good bit of this is my own, don't blame him for everything.

"One of the exercises Hendrix suggests you do if you're having trouble in your love affairs is to sit down quietly by yourself and spend a half hour or so walking mentally through your childhood. He tells you to draw a large circle on a sheet of paper and divide it in half with a horizontal line. For the first part of the exercise, you write down in the top half of the circle all the really positive sights you see on your "walk" — all the gratifying, warm-toasty moments you experienced from whoever was close to you: parents, grandparents, aunts, uncles, siblings — in short, all the good, affirmative stuff you encountered in your "primary caretakers," as the lingo calls them. Then, for the second part of the exercise, you take the walk again, this time writing down in the bottom half of the circle all the rotten, unfair, frightening, depressing experiences you had with that same group.

"The point of the exercise is twofold. For one thing, you've written out a quickie account of your whole early history, of your first and most determinative experience of *home*. All that stuff is inside you; all of it, in fact, is *you*. And what you most want in life is to find some situation in which you can feel yourself finally at home again. Consciously, of course, people usually assume they're looking only for the good stuff in their romantic hunt for home; but unconsciously — or at least less than consciously — the bad stuff is just as much a part of their choosing mechanism during the hunt. And that's the second thing: their inner compass, if you will, has two norths: both the good and the bad. The minute they start hunting, they find themselves going in conflicting directions.

37

"Now what Hendrix says is that romance — falling in love — is perhaps the greatest hunt for home in most people's lives. I myself wouldn't say that's all it is: I'm too much of a romantic to sell it that short. But it seems to me he's given a fair description of how the romantic contraption works, and why it so regularly produces the scary mistakes it does.

"Anyway, if you buy his analysis, it sheds some light on the subject. Because when you — the guy who has both the top and the bottom halves of the circle inside him — when *you* get the irresistible conviction that Jon, or whoever, is the greatest thing since the pop-up toaster, the reason is that you have finally found somebody who looks and feels like home to you. The catch, of course, is that your standard for home includes both the good and the bad you've lived through in your early years. And therefore you invariably fall in love with someone who includes those same goods and evils. Are you still with me?"

Michael smiled and said, "So far."

"Good. Now that's not to say you simply get a clone of yourself when you fall in love with somebody. That's just deceptive and dangerous nonsense. But it does mean that you get an extensive sampling of all the delights and horrors inside yourself, none of which have been permanently and perfectly reconciled in you, and all of which you're going to spend the rest of your life trying to bring into some kind of manageable peace. And therefore romance, far from being the solution to your problems, is actually a fresh situation in which you're being dragooned into facing the same old problems all over again. Or, if you want to put a good face on it, it's another chance to learn about yourself and to reconcile all the unreconciled baggage you've been carrying.

"As any given romance develops, of course, it may turn out that either you or your partner is no more able now than you were in your childhood to look the work of reconciliation straight in the eye. It may even turn out that the kindest thing you can do for each other is to pack in the whole attempt and tackle the mess some other day in a new relationship. That's always an option. But what is *not* a viable option is to think you can simply blame your partner for the failure of the romance. And you can't do that (at least not with any honesty) because the problems in the relationship were problems *you picked:* they were, in a very important sense, *you.*"

Michael interrupted. "But what about infidelity, betrayal, cheating — I don't care what you call it. He did it; I didn't. Are you seriously saying I'd go out of my way to hunt up somebody who'd do something like that to me?"

"I don't know enough about either of you to say — and you probably don't, either. But it's not the impossibility you seem to think it is. A priest friend of mine once told me about a girl he knew who had a track record of romances in which she teamed up with one bastard after another. 'She could go into the Meadowlands Stadium at halftime,' he said, 'and pick out the one guy in 60,000 people who'd beat the hell out of her.' But tell me something more important. Where did you get the idea that infidelity is the unforgivable sin?"

He looked puzzled. "Oh, I know all sins are forgivable — except the sin against the Holy Spirit, of course . . ."

I cut him off. "Who ever told you romance was the Holy Spirit? Don't answer. I'll tell you who. It was Romance herself, the Great White Queen of all our fantasies. It was the Goddess of Love, the Bright Angel whom we invite in to preside over our all-too-human love affairs and turn them into tests no mere mortal could ever pass. She's the one who talks us into swearing love and fidelity till the stars fall, even though we can't toast an English muffin right two times hand running. She's the one who made perjurers of us all. Even the church has more sense than that. It won't let you swear fidelity forever — only until you're parted by death. In marriage, infidelity is just one more sin — like burning the muffins, only more distressing. You can forgive it or not, as you like; but nobody in his right mind ever said you were bound by some angelic law not to forgive it. But in Romance with a capital *R?* Under the aegis of the Angel? Forgiveness, never. It's unthinkable, unspeakable, and undoable. And blasphemous to boot."

"Well!" Michael said. "I take it you're already up to the 'Angels' in 'ARAG' without my help. I was waiting for you to lay an unkind word on infidelity, but I guess it's too late now."

"Not really. Infidelity stinks."

"That's it?"

"No. I could go on. Infidelity hurts. Betrayal dehumanizes. Cheating lops the face off everybody it's practiced on. Shall I go on?"

"No. Because eventually there'll be a 'But.' Why don't you just go for it?"

"Right. But none of it is unforgivable as long as you're willing to lay down your life instead of punishing the offender. You want chapter and verse? *Jesus on the cross.* Period. End of tirade."

"I know," he said. "You're right."

"Then forgive him and get on with your life. And give the Angels a wide berth. They're like the camel with his nose in the tent. They find one little opening into some plain old human subject and pretty soon the whole thing collapses and suffocates you with perfectionism: the best becomes the enemy of the good, and justice becomes a recipe for bumping off the whole world. You end up with the Noah story all over again but without the merciful rainbow at the end. And all because the Angels can't die for anybody. Romance can't die for a failed lover, Marriage can't die for a straying wife, and Parenthood can't die for a wicked father. But a lover can die for a lover, a husband can die for his wife, and a child can die for her parents. The Angels *can't,* we *can,* and God *does.* That's two against one. Stick with God and yourself and you'll win."

Michael looked at his watch. "I've got to get back to work in a minute. You never got to 'Gossip.'"

"Oh, that's just a piece of boilerplate I throw in whenever anyone tells me he got rolling on some course of action because his so-called friends told him something. People always defend acting on gossip because they think gratuitous information that happens to be true isn't really gossip. But they're wrong. What gossip really is is second- or third-hand information dumped on you without either your consent or the consent of the person they tell you about. I have no idea what precise difference it would have made to you or to the relationship if the news of Jon's infidelity had come first-hand from him instead of being pumped out of him by you on the basis of gossip. But since you already knew about it and hadn't pressed the issue up to that point, it could have made a difference. Whether that difference would have been for the better or for the worse, I don't know — and neither will you, ever. But next time around, don't act on gossip. That's just a camel that gets into the tent ass-end first and craps all over everybody."

We both got up, and Michael put his arm around me. "Thanks for the uplifting lesson, Father."

"You know me," I said. "I just love technical theological terms."

FOUR

The Mystery and Forgiveness

On the analogy of an old tourist joke, "It's Tuesday, so this must be Belgium," this is an even-numbered chapter, so it must be time for you as a reader to take me to the woodshed again, this time for my counsel (or lack of it) to Michael. But since you may have felt a bit underrepresented back in Chapter Two — felt, perhaps, that because your surmised remarks came solely out of my mouth, you were being used as little more than a patsy for the advancement of my argument — let me suggest a new wrinkle for our dialogue here.

To represent you better, I'm going to introduce some new characters into this book. They will constitute a kind of Reader Advocacy Committee, and they will continue to appear on your behalf to keep me honest, thrifty, brave, clean, and reverent — or to get me into whatever other virtuous shape they think I should be whipped. They will, of course, be heavily fictionalized (as everyone in this book is, perhaps even myself); but, once again, they will be fictions based to some degree on real persons. In this instance, however, I shall tell you who my models are: they are all members of three Saturday-morning discussion groups I take part in at the parish in which I work. Their names, naturally, will be changed to protect not only their privacy but also myself, just in

42

case I guess wrong about the workings of their minds. But they're a feisty group, vociferous on almost any subject (novels, films, mysticism, religion, theology — if they had to, they could carry on for two hours about the telephone directory), so I doubt they'll object to being dragooned into service here. Indeed, since this book is scheduled to be read by them as a work in progress next April (it's now December), I'm sure that among other things they'll hazard some shrewd guesses (which I shall refuse to confirm or deny) as to who among them is who in this crew of carping critics. Without further ado, therefore, let me give you the cast of characters.

DRAMATIS PERSONAE

ALICE: a lifelong Episcopalian
OTTO: a Lover of Logic and Science
ENID: an Academic
FRANK: an evangelical Christian
LOUISE: a self-professed "Simple Person"
ROBERT: myself

ROBERT: So much for Michael and me, then; now it's your turn to have at us. Comments? Questions? Criticisms? Objections? Total disagreements? Coffee? Doughnuts? Fire away!

LOUISE: I just don't understand. I mean, I know the church is supposed to welcome sinners and forgive them, but I was surprised you never brought up the possibility that homosexuality might be a sin. Listening to you talk to Michael, it struck me that what you said was no different from what you might have said to a respectable married man who was having trouble with a wife who was cheating on him. But isn't there a difference? Isn't Michael's whole relationship with Jon wrong? Couldn't you have at least suggested that in the future he might try to avoid such relationships?

43

ROBERT: Noted. I have an idea, though. Why don't the rest of you keep pitching in? That way, we'll get a broader picture of where we're at.

OTTO: I don't agree with that at all, Louise. I'm sick and tired of the knee-jerk assumption that all sex outside the bonds of matrimony is automatically sinful. And I'll tell you why. A lot of sexual behavior outside of marriage, and certainly a lot of homosexual behavior, just boils down to mutual masturbation. Not all of it, of course, but enough to make my point. Which is that unless you're willing to say that masturbation is a nasty, wicked, sinful act (which I don't think it is; in teenagers at least, it's just a stage of development), then you shouldn't go running around giving people bad consciences about it. You or I may have gotten past that stage ourselves, but we have no right saddling others with moral hang-ups over something that probably isn't even their fault.

ENID: I've heard that objection before, Otto, but I think it misses the real point. It aims too low. Sexual acts between human beings ought not to be judged by merely physiological details, as if you were commenting on the horniness of puppy dogs. Human sexual acts have to be judged by human standards: standards like love, commitment, faithfulness. If those are present, and if *they're* made the basis of your moral judgments, as they should be, then loving, committed venereal acts between homosexuals are no different from those between heterosexuals.

LOUISE: *Venereal* acts? You mean even getting *diseases* from sex is all right?

ROBERT: No, Louise. Enid's using the correct Latin word for the subject. "Venereal" comes from *Venus,* the name of the

44

Goddess of Love; the stem of the word is actually *vener-*. "Venereal acts" are simply the physical acts involved in making love.

ENID: Yes. That's the whole point. Heterosexuals and homosexuals each make love according to their preferences. As long as what they make is love, and not cruelty, or betrayal, or exploitation, homosexuals have just as much right as heterosexuals to choose whatever venereal acts they like.

ALICE: I can see that in the case of heterosexuals; otherwise, we'd have to condemn practically every engaged couple we know. But doesn't the Bible itself condemn homosexual acts? Lord knows, there are plenty of people in the church right now who think it does. Look at the fuss over ordaining homosexual persons. Although I must say I think it sounds pretty silly coming from Episcopalians. I'm seventy, and I've known gay priests all my life — not to mention a gay bishop, who came complete with a stable of young chauffeurs.

FRANK: All that means is that the church was wrong and the Bible is right. Paul says flat out in Romans and 1 Corinthians that homosexual behavior is wrong. He says that men who "burn in their lust for one another will receive that recompense of their error which was meet." And he condemns the "effeminate" and the "abusers of themselves with mankind." Not to mention the Old Testament, Leviticus 18: "Thou shalt not lie with mankind as with womankind: it is abomination."

ENID: Well, I hope we don't get bogged down in Old Testament mores and Paul's views on sex. This book is supposedly about the Mystery of Christ. But listening to this conversation, Robert, I think you made a mistake starting out with Helen and Michael. Sex derails everything but itself. You'll be lucky

45

if you ever get to your subject. And just when I was hoping for something definitive.

ROBERT: We shall see, we shall see; but thanks for the hope. Anything more to go into the hopper?

FRANK: Yes. Quite apart from the subject of sexual sins, it seems to me that your constant reluctance to urge people to reform their lives is contrary to Scripture. I won't even quote anything, because there's just so much of it. Oh, just one, all right? Jesus forgives the woman taken in adultery, sure. And he makes it clear to her accusers that they're not to condemn her, sure. But he says to her, "Go and sin no more." Conversion comes because of forgiveness; but forgiveness without conversion of life is forgiveness misunderstood.

OTTO: I've got one more thing. I think I see what you mean by the "angelic subjects," such as romance, that we put in charge of our lives. But dragging in angels could very well involve you in almost as many irrelevancies as dragging in sex. Angels are a worn-out medieval subject: all you'll get by mentioning the word is questions about their existence instead of an understanding of what you're really trying to say.

ENID: Just one more plea for the Mystery of Christ. I agree with Otto: let's get off the irrelevancies.

ROBERT: All right, then. I've got a pageful of notes; let's see if I can make any sense of them and maybe lower some of your lifted eyebrows. Break in any time you like.

Enid, I promise you we'll get to the Mystery of Christ before the end of this chapter. But since nothing is irrelevant to that Mystery, I'm going to work my way toward it by dealing first with

46

the subjects you've all raised. Before I begin, though, I want to make an observation. One of the things you have to remember about this book is that only its odd-numbered chapters — only the actual counseling sessions — are about real-life situations. In them, you hear what I, as a reasonably responsible preacher and priest, actually say to specific persons with problems, or difficulties, or whatever. My focus in those encounters, in other words, is on the person in front of me, and not on theology, religion, or any other subject. But in these even-numbered chapters, the focus changes. The person's pain or confusion is not sitting here right in front of us. We're not talking to him or her; we're chatting away about that person (and about me) like a bunch of gossips. Our main concern is with what we ourselves think, or with what we think other people ought to think. In short, our focus here is on our own theology, opinions, and reactions, not on the person we're ostensibly talking about.

I'll grant you, of course, that this *Kaffeeklatsch* is just as much a real-life situation as any other: all our theologizing and moralizing is perfectly legitimate — for us. But I hope you'll keep in mind that you should be a little chary about faulting me for not doing in a counseling session the kind of abstract analysis we can do here.

FRANK: I don't agree with that. As a believing Christian, I think that the biggest real-life danger to Michael was the sin involved in his homosexual life-style. So I do fault you: not for your failure to do abstract analysis but for your lack of concern in not warning him against the danger of sinning. If someone you cared about was walking backward toward a cliff, you'd try to stop him, wouldn't you? How was the situation with Michael any different from that?

It's no different, Frank. It's just that the cliff I saw as the really dangerous one was different from the one you saw. The cliff I saw Michael backing toward (and that I warned him about in no uncertain terms) was not the supposedly fatal precipice of sinning, which is a "danger" only if you think sins can cut you off from the forgiveness of God in Christ; rather, it was the Grand Canyon of unforgiveness, which is the only thing (if we take the Lord's Prayer and the parable of the Unforgiving Servant seriously) that can get us in permanent Dutch with God. Admittedly, that was a judgment call on my part; but since I think there were solid Gospel reasons for making the judgment, I'm not as uncomfortable with it as you are.

Anyway, that's what I get for defending myself. The best defense is not an offense; it's to stand pat as indefensible. So back to the theological ranch. As I see things at this point, there are three topics I want to say something about: homosexuality, angels, and romance — in that order, because given the concerns you've just raised, it seems to be the only route left to get us to Enid's concern for the Mystery.

The topic of homosexuality, as far as I'm concerned, makes for a rather bumpy detour to the Mystery of Christ. But since I invited you to turn onto it by introducing you to Michael in the first place, I owe you at least something about it as an abstract subject. There are two reasons why I didn't bring it up in the conversation you overheard. The first, as I mentioned, is that he and I had already discussed it on other occasions. But the second and far more important reason is that when I'm counseling, I never let myself get trapped in discussions of whether something — x, or y, or z — is or isn't a sin. All that ever does is distract counselees' minds from the main subject — namely, the forgiveness they already have through the indwelling of the Mystery of Christ. It just encourages them in their inveterate habit of thinking that the Christian life consists essentially of identifying no-nos and avoiding them. Which is dead wrong on two counts. One, it's simply a thinly disguised version of the notion that we can be saved by what we do rather than by the grace of God alone. And two, it's baloney, because there is no way we, as members of a fallen race, can ever get sin out of our lives by our own efforts; only God can do that. So when I'm counseling, I simply refuse to talk about the sinfulness of any particular human act. And here I'm going to talk about it only if you promise to remember this: for as long as we're on the subject of the sinfulness (or not) of homosexuality, we will be temporarily leaving the great subject of God's free gift in Christ in order to muck about in the distinctly two-bit subjects of morality and ethics. Okay?

FRANK: But doesn't the Bible make it clear that we are to at least try to avoid sin? And doesn't *that* mean that we're duty-bound to be clear about what is and isn't sinful?

My answer to that, Frank, is no — at least not if you read the Bible as a grace-filled whole instead of a divinely sanctioned sin sheet. But since (albeit under protest) I'm going to spend some time on how abstract ethics decides whether homosexuality is or isn't sinful, I'm going to ask you to bear with me while we wallow in the dismal swamp of moral theology.

First of all, when Christians start making ethical judgments about homosexuality, they are not, strictly speaking, making those judgments on the basis of Scripture alone: they, like all human beings, are making them on the basis of the general principles of moral reasoning. That's why homosexuality is a large and easily muddled subject — and why Christians express the same diametrically opposed views on it as everybody else. Some think it's sinful; others think it isn't. (I myself happen to think it's not.) Some think the handful of biblical passages that condemn it resolve the question; others think either that the condemnations in those passages are based on social circumstances that no longer apply, or that the moral principles behind them are too narrow to fit in with the Christian insistence on love as the great commandment. (Once again, I land on the side of the "others.")

But whatever position you take on the matter, it's essential to remember that the answer you give to an ethical question depends very much on how you set up the question. If (as I and Enid do, for example) you take the point of view that homosexual venereal acts *within a loving, committed relationship* are legitimate expressions of sexuality (a view usually referred to as the "situation ethic" approach), then obviously you don't call them sinful, since the love and commitment have legitimized them for you. Or again, if you think homosexuality as such is an inherited disposition about which a person has no choice (once more, I tend to agree), then you don't call that a sin, either: you may consider it to be sad, or bad, or a condition that needs therapy, but it isn't something either you or a just God can *blame* someone for. And the same thing is true if you decide it's a disposition foisted on young people by the depredations of seducers or by the psychological shortcomings of their parents: nobody can be blamed for a condition that he or she didn't willingly create. Clearly, then (to sum up the essential moral reasoning by which this abstract discussion of "sinfulness" has so far operated), neither homosexuality nor homosexual venereal acts can be seen as sinful unless, first, such a state or such acts are held to be evil and, second, they are freely and knowingly chosen by the person involved. Unless *both* conditions are met, no moral culpability can be assigned to *any* human being, let alone to homosexuals.

On the other hand, if you approach the morality of sexual acts from what is usually called the "natural law" point of view, you can just as easily end up condemning not just homosexuality but *all* venereal acts other than intercourse in the missionary position between male and female marriage partners. Since this is a family book, I shall leave you to imagine for yourselves the rather wide range of sexual acts proscribed by this approach. The only thing I will mention here is my personal conviction that touting such a system of thought as the only "natural law" approach begs the question. *All* rational ethical systems argue on the basis of natural law; they differ from each other only over *which particular principle of natural law* should be made the primary principle of ethics. "Situation ethic" systems opt for *love* as the governing consideration; the erroneously labeled "natural law" approach tends to focus on the *naturalness* or *unnaturalness* of specific venereal acts. But both make their judgments by looking to some dimension of *human nature* as the standard for defining what is right or wrong for human beings.

Enough of this moral wrangling, though: each of us has paid his ethical money and made his moral choice. All we can reasonably do on the level of the scholastic morality game is either respect each other's choice (even if we don't agree with it), or try to argue each other out of the positions we've so far bought. But for as long as we insist on playing such a game, that's the best we can expect.

So let me quit the sport of abstract ethics and get back to my objection to even discussing the "sinfulness" of homosexuality or anything else. From a biblical and theological point of view, that whole approach to the human condition begs two very important questions. First, it assumes that sinning is simply a conscious, voluntary bit of business that we could avoid if only we would make the effort — if only we would just obey the Law of God, and thus render ourselves sinless. And second, it assumes that such self-acquired sinlessness has been stipulated by God as the essential precondition of his favor toward us.

Both of those assumptions, however, are dead wrong not only theologically but scripturally. To see the error in the first one, go back and read Romans 7: that's the chapter in which Paul most clearly insists that sin is an indwelling condition we can't get rid of by any effort of our own, and which even the Law of God, in all its holiness, righteousness, and goodness, only aggravates. We are, he says, "sold under sin" — helpless slaves of it, not the masters of our fate that scholastic ethics implies we are. And to see the error in the second assumption, take a look at Romans 5:8: that's where Paul says that God "proves his love for us in that *while we were still sinners* Christ died for us" — thus scotching once and for all any notion that God has made sinlessness on our part a condition of his grace.

So the theological upshot of all this is pretty much a draw. If homosexual acts are sinful, you're still not allowed to run around pretending that God can't or won't forgive homosexual persons unless they abstain from such acts; and if they're not sinful, but still repugnant to you, you're not allowed by common decency to make your tastes the standard for other people's behavior. Either way, your first duty is to love such people *as they are* and not to imply that God has given you permission to hold an axe over their heads. Because if God has really done what the Epistle to the Romans says he has, he's gone ahead and solved all his problems with sin independently of what sinners might or might not do about it.

That's outrageous, of course; and it's not at all what most people think a God who's a card-carrying member of the God Union ought to do. But it is what the Mystery of Christ is all about. Because by that Mystery, God's love and forgiveness are intimately and immediately present in full force to everyone in the world, virtuous or wicked, Christian or not, simply because the Word of God incarnate in Jesus is present to everyone in the world. Nobody has to clean up his act in order to be forgiven or loved; all anybody has to do is *believe (trust, have faith)* that he's home free already, and then enjoy the forgiveness he's had all along by passing it on to everybody he runs into. Therefore, the only *unforgivable* act, if there is such a thing, is refusing to be forgiven or to forgive — which is not so much a sin as it is a failure of *faith*. Everything else has been taken care of.

ENID: I don't know about anyone else, but I've had about enough ethics and morals to last me a lifetime. If we still have to slog through angels and romance, can't we at least just get on with it? Otto may be worried that you think angels actually exist, but I'm worried that if you get on the subject of romance

52

again, you'll never get to the Mystery of Christ. Let's move
it!

Thank you, Enid. With that flick of the riding crop, off we
go to the angels. Otto, I'm not in the least concerned with the
question of whether they actually exist. That can't be either proved
or disproved by abstract thought, any more than the existence of
dogs, cats, or dragons can. The only way we can prove *existence* is
by physical evidence, not by a priori argument. And since physical
evidence of angels is by definition unavailable, so is proof or
disproof. So if you want to write them off as a flight of medieval
fancy, feel free to do so. I do have one comment, though, on your
objection to them: it sounds a bit strange coming from a twentieth-century human being. Think about it. *Star Trek* is still selling
like hotcakes. Science fiction's great stock-in-trade is "alien species."
And perfectly serious thinkers (not to mention cocktail party
philosophers) love to beat up on Christianity because they find
our belief that God reconciled the whole creation by becoming
human nothing more than arrogant chauvinism on the part of a
two-bit species. You've heard them: "Really, now; there are probably
[they mean, of course, *possibly*] hundreds of intelligent species out
there in other galaxies, many of them no doubt [again, *possibly*]
more advanced than we are."

Well, for my money, that's chauvinism on the part of the
two-bit modern age, or else it's ignorance of what earlier generations were actually saying. When the Bible or the medieval church
talked about angels, they were talking precisely about the vast
variety of creatures God has made: about what they thought of as
the *scala creationis,* the "ladder of creation." Angels happened to
be above us on the ladder, just as frogs and ducks happened to be
below us: they were our big brothers, so to speak, just as the
so-called lower orders were our little brothers. All we've done by
getting rid of angels is to substitute for some really splendid and
interesting creatures a bunch of usually ugly characters who look

53

and act suspiciously like human beings walking around in tin cans or badly made bodies. Think of R2D2, of Lieutenant Worf, of Mr. Spock, of Lieutenant Commander Data, or even of Jabba the Hutt. I'm not sure what they all prove psychologically or philosophically; but they do seem to indicate that the theological thirst of human beings for "big brothers," both good and bad, is just as much a modern as a medieval trait. That proves nothing, of course. But it does bear witness that such creatures are hardly a worn-out notion. Obi-Wan Kenobi is a dead ringer for the Archangel Michael, and Jabba the Hutt is a pretty good stand-in for Satan. The ladder of creation is still firmly propped in our minds.

As a matter of fact, the business of good and bad angels brings me right to what I really want to say about "the angelic" as it influences human affairs, and to what lay behind my remarks to Michael on the subject. One of the surprising twists in the history of thought in this century has been the recovery by theologians of the category of *the angelic,* and specifically of the "fallen" version of it, *the demonic.* By the late nineteenth and early twentieth centuries, most up-to-date theological types had simply trashed the whole idea of angels and demons: it was unscientific, it was mere folklore, it was just old baggage that Victorian idealism, the doctrine of evolution, the discovery of relativity, and the invention of the internal combustion engine had rendered unnecessary.

But then came World War I, and then the extermination of the Jews under Nazism, and finally World War II with its atomic denouement. Suddenly, the idea that humanity was "every day, in every way, getting better and better" came crashing down around our ears. The theologians, therefore, had a crisis of ideas. How, they asked themselves, could they reconcile their habitual belief in progress with the obvious fact that these horrors were perpetrated by the most progressive folks on earth? Well, the answer was, they couldn't; so, to their credit, they did a fast reverse and cut back to *the demonic.* If people who kissed their children goodnight and sang them to sleep could go to the office in the morning and schedule two trainloads of Jews for Auschwitz, they must have gotten themselves in league with something more, and also something terrifyingly less, than human. Accordingly, the theologians decided that what had seduced such people was a "fallen" angelic principle (the "demon" of a purely Aryan race) that offered them the vision of a perfect world available at bargain rates. "Only one more war," it whispered; "only the already despised non-Aryan races to be gotten rid of." In short, the theologians turned to the idea of the demonic in order to explain why "good" people could so easily end up doing bad things.

Now, for one thing, I find that revival of the theological concept of the demonic a refreshing breath of realism after all the optimistic hogwash of our immediate forebears. Good people have always been able to be led into bad actions if you could convince them that some "higher purpose" was being served. We are suckers for the angelic/demonic pitch. Taken as individuals, for example, all the members of the vestry of this parish would be perfectly able to forgive and/or understand the simple fact that one of their priests was guilty of something shady (you pick it: a hand in the till, an affair with a soprano, a real estate scam). Not only that, but they would all know in their hearts that forgiveness and understanding, not condemnation and ostracism, were exactly what Jesus had enjoined upon them. But as *The Vestry,* assembled in solemn conclave under the aegis of the Angel of *The Parish,* what would they do? Well, you know the answer to that as well as I do: they would serve him or her up to the Bishop on a platter and do everything they could to run the offender out of town on a rail. And do you know why? Because while each one of them could conceivably lay down his or her life for the priest, there is no way in heaven or on earth that the Angel they serve can lay down its life for anybody. The Angel is deathless, immortal; mere mortals who get in its way have to be sacrificed.

But, for another thing, I find it odd that the theologians of "the demonic" didn't go all the way and inveigh just as much against the

55

"good" angels as the "bad" ones. It seems to me that the problem with the human race is not the occasional games it plays with the wrong angels but its inveterate hankering to play in the angelic league at all. It strikes me that it is precisely the spiritual nobility of the angelic institutions and entities to which we give power over our lives (but which will never lay down *their* lives for us) that is the deepest root of our troubles. Nations, States, Corporations — and all the other sovereign abstractions like Romance, Motherhood, and Friendship — are the very things to whose immortal interests we sacrifice what is best and most human about us.

Take Romance, for example. According to the old bromide, infidelity is not necessarily the end of a marriage, but it's always the end of a romance. Do you know why that is? It's because a romance is much more of an Angel than a marriage is. Marriage is a practical arrangement between two people. Even in the marriage rite itself, the church never once asks the parties if they love each other, let alone if they love each other with an all-consuming fervor that will last till the stars fall. It only asks them if they are *determined* to love, comfort, honor, and keep each other, all of which are down-to-earth, practical activities. And it expressly limits the term of those activities to "as long as you both shall live" — which, even if they turn out to live to a hundred, is well short of forever. It asks them, in short, to say "I will" to a limited number of realistic promises; it does not (except in the movies) ask them to say "I do" to a lot of overinflated, eternal claims.

In Romance, however, it's precisely those high-flown, "spiritual" claims that lovers rattle on endlessly about — not, please note, because their primary care is for each other as human beings (though they think it is), but because each one of them cares secretly and most of all for the Angel of Romance. Are you aware, though, of just how much the Angel of Romance cares about human beings? It doesn't care about *them* at all. It cares only about their perfection as lovers: about how intensely they long for each other, about how luxuriously the weed of their longing grows

56

during their separations, and, above all, about how perfectly they are willing to die of that longing. Not only will it not lay down its own life for them; it does not even want them to die for *each other* (as one of them might do, perhaps, in rescuing the other from a burning building). Rather, its profoundest wish is that they should die of an essentially self-regarding preoccupation with *longing as such* so they can be liberated, as Romance itself is, from the inconveniences of a life as real beings in a real world. Or, as Auden so vividly put it, so they can be free at last "from these helpless agglomerations of dishevelled creatures with their bed-wetting, vomiting, weeping bodies, their giggling, fugitive, disappointing hearts, and scrawling, blotted, misspelt minds, to whom we have so foolishly tried to bring the light they did not want."

At its root, therefore, Romance is always a love affair with death. In its purity, it always says that dying of love is the ultimate perfection of love — that dropping dead of desire is the ultimate avenue to "spiritual" perfection. In the best romances of Western literature, as a matter of fact, the two lovers die together in each other's arms without ever having enjoyed the physical consummation of their love. And those are the best romances precisely because the only thing the Angel is interested in (namely, the love, not the lovers) is the only thing left on stage when the curtain comes down. The Angel cares only that we be in love with Love and, above all, in love with Death: it cares not a fig whether we are actually loving, comforting, or honoring to each other. And that, Virginia, is why infidelity in a romantic love affair must always result in the extermination of the relationship, and why forgiveness is never an option: when one of the parties to a romance messes around with somebody else, that party must simply be bumped off. If the Angel can't get its orgy of liberation from matter through a death of ardent longing, it will still get death into the act any way it can. Forgiveness, which would be a kind, practical, life-affirming thing for one party to give the other, is simply out of the question.

All of which brings us back again to the Mystery of Christ,

the Mystery of the Incarnation of God in merely human flesh. When the God revealed in Christ redeems and reconciles the world, he does something totally unromantic. He does not take on angelic nature; look at the Letter to the Hebrews (2:16-17):

> For it is clear that he did not come to help angels, but the descendants of Abraham. Therefore he had to become like his brothers and sisters in every respect, so that he might be a merciful and faithful high priest in the service of God, to make a sacrifice of atonement for the sins of the people.

Do you see what that means? It means that God's action in the world takes place entirely in plain old messed-up human nature. He does not kill off sinners; rather, he himself dies a totally human death in order that they may live new and fully human lives in the power of his resurrection. Accordingly, Romance is not just a perfectionist, life-denying activity that leads sinners (the only available candidates for the role of lovers) to beat up on each other. It's also a religion in its own right, and a purely "spiritual" religion at that: one that stands in flat contradiction to the Gospel of the Incarnation. Because the Incarnation says that God cares more about having us in relationship with himself than he does about the purity of his love. It says that he is in love with *us*, not with his romantic love for us. And it produces not a religion that will sooner or later cut off all its adherents but the outrageously Good News that God will give up anything he has just so he can have us.

And once you see that (namely, the primacy of God's insistence on keeping us in a life-affirming relationship with himself), everything we've been talking about in this discussion begins to light up. Take the Law in the Old Testament, for instance. Everyone talks about it as if it's some third person standing outside of or in between God and us — as if we and God are looking at each other not in a relationship of care but over both our shoulders at a prosecutor called the Commandments who tells God to hate us

58

and us to fear God. But if you actually read the Old Testament, the Law isn't presented that way at all. It's presented as a Covenant, a *relationship* between God and his people. Sure, the people break the Covenant; and sure, God tells them in no uncertain terms that they're messing up royally. But from Genesis to Malachi (and from Matthew to Revelation under the New Covenant), God never considers canceling the relationship because of the messes. Just once, at the beginning of the story of Noah, he toys with the idea; but before the story ends, he says flatly he's never going to consider it again. Look at what he finally says in Genesis 9:11-13:

"I establish my covenant with you, that never again shall all flesh be cut off by the waters of a flood, and never again shall there be a flood to destroy the earth." God said, "This [the Rainbow] is the sign of the covenant that I make between me and you and every living creature that is with you, for all future generations: I have set my bow in the clouds, and it shall be a sign of the covenant between me and the earth."

And even when the Law as such is given on Mt. Sinai, it stands first and foremost as a witness to the covenant relationship of God to his people and not as a prosecuting third party bent on setting them against each other. Once again, look at the text (Exod. 24:7-8):

Then he took the book of the covenant, and read it in the hearing of the people; and they said, "All that the LORD has spoken we will do, and we will be obedient." Moses took the blood and dashed it on the people, and said, "See the blood of the covenant that the LORD has made with you in accordance with all these words."

And finally, when God perfects his relationship with humanity in the New Covenant, he does it by proclaiming that he has died and risen for it so that we as his beloved, our sins notwithstanding, may live with him as his bride and his wife. The final image in the Bible, you see, is not some romantic, pining, non-relationship of lovers in love with Love but the ultimate in domestic coziness: the *marriage* of God and creation as a result of the Incarnation of the Word of God. The whole passage (in Revelation 21:1-4) is worth quoting (italics mine):

> Then I saw a new heaven and *a new earth;* for the first heaven and the first earth had passed away, and the sea was no more. And I saw the holy city, the new Jerusalem, coming down out of heaven from God, *prepared as a bride adorned for her husband.* And I heard a loud voice from the throne saying, "See, *the home of God is among mortals.* He will dwell with them as their God; they will be his peoples, and God himself will be with them; he will wipe every tear from their eyes. *Death will be no more;* mourning and crying and pain will be no more, for the first things have passed away."

ENID: I hate to break in again with the same old song, but do you think that perhaps *now* we could get to the Mystery of Christ?

Yes, Enid. At last, yes. Let me tie all of this up for you with what will probably turn out to be a longish piece of string. The beginning of the string will be a new image of how the Mystery of Christ actually restores the relationship between God and us; the end will be something about the centrality of faith to our enjoyment of the relationship. In between, I'll simply try to keep the knots to a minimum.

I want you to think of the Mystery of God's Incarnation in the world (as proclaimed and sacramentalized in Jesus) in terms of what the director of a piece of improvisational "street theater" does when he attempts to make a coherent play out of the random and often senseless actions his "cast" may offer him. First of all, like such a director, the divine, directing Mystery does not stand outside the action of history holding a script and telling everyone to stick to it. Instead, the Word of God Incarnate (God himself) enters the play of history in person, not as an interfering angel with his own agenda but as a human being among human beings. He abrogates nothing the various actors want to do; he uses no force, no coercion, to get them to do what he wants. Mary is free, Peter is free, Judas is free, Pilate is free, you are free, I am free: every one of us can do whatever he or she wants. The divine Director does, of course, guarantee that the play will have a happy ending (it is, after all, a Divine Comedy). But that ending will not be dictated by plausible or pushy interventions on his part. Rather, he will achieve it out of the cast's actions by a combination of paradox, hands-off body English, and, when necessary, the sequestering of all the possible unhappiness in the play in himself.

Second, therefore, he enters the play *as it is,* and he enters it in a way that is unrecognizable as the action of a respectable, directing God. On the evidence of the actual history of the play, in fact, he is indistinguishable from the characters of the play — with one notable exception, which is that he stands at all times against the other characters' preoccupation with *religion.* And the reason for that is that it's precisely their religions and their religiosity that keep their actions from reaching a happy ending. It's their bondage to angelic notions and their worship of false gods that prevent any truly human successes from coming off. And if you think for a moment about this refusal on the part of the Director to have any truck with religion, you will see that it is one of the hallmarks of Jesus' actions. Who in fact did he spend most of his time inveighing against? Sinners? No; he was accused of being too friendly with sinners and even of being one himself: a glutton, a winebibber, and a blasphemer. Those he really socked it to were the respectable religionists, scribes, Pharisees, practitioners of the Law, and hypocrites.

LOUISE: But didn't he finally do something religious when he died on the cross?

I'm sorry to disappoint you, Louise, but no again. Nothing he did was in any way recognizable as having religious significance. He died as a common criminal. The cross is a sign not of sacrifice but of execution — of a nasty bit of judicial murder that has no more intrinsic significance than the thousands of other such acts all through history. To be sure, people have turned the cross into a religious symbol; but since Christianity is not a "religion," that sort of thing can only lead to confusion. Christianity is the proclamation of the end of religion, not of a new religion, or even of the best of all possible religions. And therefore if the cross is the sign of anything, it's the sign that God has gone out of the religion business and solved all the world's problems without requiring a single human being to do a single religious thing. What the cross is actually a sign of is the fact that religion can't do a thing about the world's problems — that it never did work and it never will — which is exactly what Hebrews 10:4 says: "For it is impossible for the blood of bulls and goats to take away sins." So, if you want to theologize it into a sign, the best you can do is say that it's the sign of the fulfillment of all that religion ever tried to do and couldn't. The fact that the death of Jesus was non-religious says that loud and clear. And the fact that we put up crosses in the church, and make the sign of the cross on those who are baptized, says the same thing.

If that's hard for you to grasp, try a little mental exercise with me. Suppose for a moment that the work of Jesus — the manifestation of the whole Mystery of God's Incarnation — was taking place now rather than in the first century. Suppose that the *Jesus* in whom he became human had been born in an inner city to poor, Hispanic parents in 1959, that he began teaching when he was about thirty, and that after three years he ran afoul of the authorities and was condemned to death in 1992. Then ask yourself, How would he be executed? Most likely, of course, he'd die in the electric chair.

But then, jump ahead to the year 3092 and ask yourself another question: What would his followers in that distant future be doing with that manner of death in terms of ecclesiastical symbolism? It's interesting, isn't it? The chosen sign of the saving Mystery of his death would be not a cross but an electric chair. There would be replicas of the Old Rugged Electric Chair in all the churches. Solid brass ones, fourteen-karat gold-on-silver ones, fabulous diamond-encrusted ones on cathedral altars, tiny silver-chained ones to wear around your neck, and even molded chocolate ones for Easter candy. Not only that, but those who were baptized would probably have their heads shaved and be strapped into a chair for the rite.

But perhaps that's enough to make my point about the cross. All I want to add here is that Jesus' resurrection from the dead was just as non-religious. Nobody at all saw him actually do it. And only a handful of people witnessed the empty tomb — a witness that was written off by a good many others as a fraud. True enough, his followers claimed to have seen him risen; but he didn't bother to stay around long enough to get any decent publicity. Instead, he disappeared after forty days and left a ragtag group of apostles and disciples to proclaim that this festival of irreligious mysteriousness was in fact the best news the human race had ever had. Weird; definitely weird. But not religious.

Third and finally, though, think of how the street-theater director's cast of characters might try to explain to themselves how he finally turned their hodgepodge of actions into a play with a happy ending. They might, of course, attribute his success to specific bits of intervention on his part: a word here, the suggestion of a different bit of business there. And, true enough, each of those interventions would have been an instance of the director himself entering into the interchanges of the play. But if the cast were wise, they would look deeper than that. For one thing, they would see that since the key to the play's success didn't lie *in them,* it had in some sense to have been *in the director* all along. And for another thing, they would realize that since the success of the play was caused by the director, he had to have been in the play *at every moment of its action,* not just at the times they could recognize as his interventions.

In other words, they would have to invent something very like the notion of *mystery* to explain his constant, unobservable presence throughout the play; and they would have to invent something very like the notion of *sacrament* to explain how his occasional, specific actions were not just single instances of his acting to make the play a success but rather manifestations, in certain situations, of his real and effective presence to the play all along. Or, to put it another way, they would have to develop a *directology* (read "theology") of his work that met two important criteria. On the one hand, it would have to affirm his intimate and immediate relationship to every moment of the play and not insist that his specific interventions were the whole cause of its happy ending. On the other hand, it would have to affirm his general relationship to the play in such a way that it didn't deny the real presence and effectiveness of that relationship in his specific interventions.

Which brings us (luckily, because the analogy is just about to wear thin and break down) to what the church at its best has done in developing a *theology* (read "directology") of the work of God incarnate in the world. Needless to say, the church's theologizing has had its share of analogous temptations. Some theologians leaned in the direction of the "on the one hand" in the preceding paragraph. They treated the death and resurrection of God in Christ, for example, as if it were the only time and place in the history of creation where God had done his reconciling work. He acted once and for all, they said, in A.D. 29. Taken literally, of course, that got them into trouble. The "once" made it sound as if God had been absent from the play of history until he showed

64

up after the intermission and did his thing in Jesus. And the "for all" gave them problems because it required a lot of legalistic shuffling to get the job he did in Jesus applied to the characters who died before the intermission, or to those who did their part in the play of history in places that Jesus (or his church) never got to before they died — or never got to at all.

This approach also led them to take a highly "transactional" view of what the church was up to. The church, for them, became the pipeline through which the work of God in Christ was funneled to the world. If you got yourself connected to the church, you got the happy ending; if you didn't, you were out of luck. Or, to change the illustration, the church took the God in Christ who said he was the Light of the world and turned him into the Lighting Company of the world, complete with access fees (lots of good deeds) to be paid before you could tap into his power, and the threat of a cutoff in service if you didn't keep up the monthly payments with righteous acts. But if Jesus really shines as the Light of the world the way the sun shines as the light of the earth, then nobody needs to do anything to get the light. The Mystery of Christ shines from one end of creation to the other: the whole shooting match is already lit up everywhere, free for nothing. The church doesn't have to tear around telling people to get themselves wired into Jesus. It just has to bring them the hilariously Good News that if only they will trust Jesus and open their eyes, the darkness will be gone. And it will be gone because, except for the blindness of their unbelief, it was never there at all.

The whole, reconciling work of God incarnate in Jesus, you see, is already in everybody and everything by the universal presence of the Mystery of Christ. Therefore, the church is *catholic* not because it has the whole human race inside it (it never has had, and it probably never will) but because it is the sign (sacrament) to the world of the catholic reconciliation God has handed to every last human being from Adam to whomever. And do you see what *that* means? It means that the Mystery of Christ is present not just in Christians or in good guys but present in sinners right in the midst of their sins. It means that the Mystery isn't something that picks up its lily-white skirts and runs away when somebody does a no-no. The Mystery just hangs around everywhere: it's in the murderer at the moment he puts the knife in the victim's chest; it's in the victim as the knife punctures her heart — and it's in the abuser and the abused, the torturer and the tortured, the violator and the violated. You don't earn its presence by being a good egg, and you can't lose it by being a bad one.

Which is why, I suppose, when God chose to sacramentalize the presence of that Mystery in Jesus between 4 B.C. and A.D. 29, he made sure it got manifested in a very questionable egg indeed. In some sense, to be sure, Christians are committed to take seriously the notion that Jesus was "without sin." But you have to be very careful not to turn him into a Little Lord Fauntleroy in velvet pants. Because whatever the theological significance of his "sinlessness" may be, it's a cinch that the notion would have been news to most of the people who ran into him during his career. As a matter of fact, a lot of them just lumped him together with the whores and tax sharks he habitually hung around with and let it go at that. Even more alarmingly, he never even tried to convince them otherwise — being content, it would seem, to be made "like his brothers and sisters in every respect," even to the point of being a rotten egg, or, in Paul's more elegant but even more astounding phrase, of being "made sin for us" (2 Cor. 5:21).

The Mystery of Christ manifested in Jesus, therefore, is the Mystery of the *irrevocable marriage of God to creation* — of a completely restored relationship "for better for worse, for richer for poorer, in sickness and in health." It is not some divine Romance with an idealized beloved; it's the embracing of all the gorgeousness and grisliness of the world because that's all the world God wants and all he's got — because "the gifts and the calling of God are irrevocable" (Rom. 11:29), and because, as the omnipotent, champion turkey-caller of all time, he doesn't quit till he

66

gets every turkey in the world: Robert, Louise, Otto, Enid, Alice, and Frank; Alexander the Terrible, Sam the Serial Killer, and Geoffrey the Office Letch; St. Francis of Assisi, St. Gregory the Great, and St. Jerome the Professional Grouch — and even St. George the Dragon-slayer, just in case he had the dumb luck actually to exist. We are all the Bride, the Wife of the Lamb who is the Light of a world made new in his death and resurrection.

I promised you that at the end of this long string I would give you something about the centrality of faith to the enjoyment of the Mystery of God's Incarnation, of your restored relationship in the Marriage of God to creation. Here it is; read it slowly, because it will be over in just two short sentences:

You don't have to work for the relationship because you've got it already. Just trust Jesus and open your eyes.

FIVE

Dan

The conversation you're about to overhear in this chapter will be a bit different from the ones I've let you in on so far. It took place not during a leisurely office visit but in less than five minutes on a Sunday morning after the main service at the church. Dan (his name is all I'm going to tell you about him) waited until everyone else had shaken hands with the clergy at the door and then zeroed in on me about the contents of my sermon that day.

But before I give you the conversation, I think I should preface it with two background items: the text of the New Testament reading on which the sermon was based, and a copy of the notes from which I preached. (I almost never preach from a written-out manuscript, so these notes — tidied up and extended somewhat, but otherwise unchanged — are all I have as a record of what I said.) The fact that I haven't undertaken to reconstruct the sermon at length should be looked on not simply as a labor-saving break for myself but as a favor to you: making people read published sermons is a form of torture that went out of style with the death of Queen Victoria. So on with the preliminaries, and then straight into the dialogue.

(The words and phrases in bold type
are the ones commented on in the sermon.)

³Blessed be the God and Father of our Lord Jesus Christ, who has blessed us in Christ with every spiritual blessing in the heavenly places, ⁴just as **he chose us in Christ before the foundation of the world** to be holy and blameless before him in love. ⁵**He destined us for adoption as his children** through Jesus Christ, according to the good pleasure of his will, ⁶**to the praise of his glorious grace that he freely bestowed on us in the Beloved.** ⁷In him we have redemption through his blood, the forgiveness of our trespasses, according to the riches of his grace ⁸that he lavished on us. With all wisdom and insight ⁹he has made known to us **the mystery of his will,** according to his good pleasure **that he set forth in Christ,** ¹⁰as a **plan for the fullness of time, to gather up all things in him,** things in heaven and things on earth. ¹¹**In Christ we have also obtained an inheritance,** having been **destined according to the purpose of him who accomplishes all things according to his counsel and will,** ¹²so that we, who were the first to set our hope on Christ, might live for the praise of his glory. ¹³In him you also, when you had heard the word of truth, the gospel of your salvation, and had believed in him, were marked with the seal of the promised Holy Spirit; ¹⁴this is the pledge of our inheritance toward redemption as God's own people, to the praise of his glory.

¹⁵I have heard of your **faith** in the Lord Jesus and your love toward all the saints, and for this reason ¹⁶I do not cease to give thanks for you as I remember you in my prayers. ¹⁷I pray that the God of our Lord Jesus Christ, the Father of glory, may give you a spirit of wisdom and revelation as you come to know him, ¹⁸so that, with the eyes of your heart enlightened, you may know

69

what is the hope to which he has called you, what are the riches of his glorious inheritance among the saints, [19]and what is the immeasurable greatness of his power for us who **believe**. . . .

(The materials in and following the words in boxes are illustrations.)

✝ 2 Xmas C: Ephesians 1:3-19

THE INCARNATION AS THE GIFT OF UNIVERSAL ACCEPTANCE IN CHRIST

HOW does the gift of Incarnation extend itself to us? How does salvation in our Lord Jesus Christ work?

Models:

HS Yearbook This model holds that salvation works by **our remembering** what God did for us in Jesus and then trying to pattern our lives accordingly. It says that just as when we look at a **high school yearbook**, we put ourselves back into "contact" with those we knew then, so we put ourselves into "saving contact" with Jesus by **recalling** the nice things he's done for us and being inspired by them to change our behavior. This model is **N.G.** from start to finish. First of all, it's **N.G.** because **remembering** persons from the past is not the same thing as being in actual contact with them. Second, it's **N.G.** because it implies that we, **by our act of remembering,** are the ultimate **agents** of our salvation. And finally, it's **N.G.** because it underestimates the **problem of Sin**: namely, the fact that no matter how much we may **think** about niceness, or how hard we may **try** to be nice, **we** can't cure the problem of the endemic "un-niceness" of the human race.

Ticket Window This model holds that we're saved because the Word incarnate in Jesus is the official seller of tickets to the "Heavenly Stadium" and that he sells them to those who have the moral or spiritual "purchase price." It implies, in other words, that salvation is a **commercial transaction**. This model is **O.K.** because it posits God in Christ as the only one who can get us into the Stadium; but it's **N.G.** because it makes some **earning power** on our part the precondition for a ticket's actually getting into our hands.

Stadium open to all for free This model holds that we're saved because **everybody** has not only been given a free ticket by the presence of the Incarnate Word to **everybody** via the **Mystery of Christ** but has also, by that same Mystery, actually been put into the Stadium and been given free beer, banners, and hot dogs. **This model is the only one that's O.K. on all counts.** First, it's the only one that's supported by Jesus' **parables of grace** — THE KING'S SON'S WEDDING; THE GREAT BANQUET; THE LABORERS IN THE VINEYARD: in these, **acceptance** is by **grace**, not **works**. And, as portrayed in these parables, that acceptance **precedes all history**, whether our own or the world's: God **"chose us in Christ before the foundation of the world."** It calls for no merit or work on our part — only **faith**. Second, it's the only model that's truly **catholic**, that gets (as Jesus claimed to get — "I, when I am lifted up from the earth, will draw all people to myself") **everybody** into the Stadium (except, of course, those who refuse to accept the free beer, etc.). Third, it's the only model that emphasizes (as the parables do) the fact that salvation is a **party thrown for everybody**, not just a reward for the ethically affluent.

71

Summary to this point: The **Incarnation**, accordingly, is a Mystery that is true **all through history**. Jesus is the **great sacrament** of that Mystery, the **real presence** of it in his historical time and place. But the Mystery of the Word incarnate in Jesus is also really and effectively present at **all times and places** because that Word is **God himself**, the second Person of the Trinity. In Jesus, the Mystery didn't **show up** in a world from which it was previously absent; rather, **what had been there all along** was finally and fully **manifested** in him.

Now: Let's progress through the text of the reading:

1. *Verse 4: exelexato = chose:* "He **chose** us in Christ **before the foundation of the world**" — before **we** did anything about responding:

    Predestination to life is a witness to the **free inclusion** of all. (We should stay away from any notion of **reprobation**, of **predestination to damnation** — it's the answer to a question that should never be asked: the only thing we need to know is that our reward has nothing to do with merit or demerit.)

2. *Verse 5: huiothesia = adoption, sonship:* "he destined us for **adoption as his children**":

    We are made **children** (sons) by having **the Sonship of the Son** effectively declared over us by the Word of God from the beginning of creation.

3. *Verse 6: charis = grace:* "to the praise of his glorious **grace**":

    The adoption is a **favor**, a **free gift**; as above, it is unmerited — and it precedes all of the history of the world.

4. *Verses 9 & 10: mysterion = mystery:* "the **mystery** of his will . . . as a plan for the fullness of time":

    The gift is **hidden**, but **hidden** under **signs, sacraments** that manifest its real presence; the signs are: first **Christ**, then **the church**, and then **the sacraments of the church**.

5. *Verse 10: anakephalaiosis = recapitulation,* new chapter, heading up, gathering up: "to **gather up** all things in him":

    In the Mystery of Christ the Word of God makes a **new creation**, a whole **new start** for the world; Christ is, and always was, and always will be the **head** of creation; he redeems and reconciles **this world** — he does not junk it and drag us off to some purely "spiritual" heaven.

6. *Verses 15-19: pistis = faith:* "I have heard of your **faith** . . . power for us who **believe**":

    Believing is the way we relate ourselves to the gift; **it is not a condition of the gift's being given**. Faith (trust in Jesus, not just intellectual assent) is the acceptance of a **gift already given by a person**; it must not be turned into a **work on our part that earns us brownie points**.

Final Summary: Romans 8:1: "**There is therefore now no condemnation for those who are in Christ Jesus.**" Everybody in the **world** is in Jesus by virtue of the indwelling Mystery of Christ; the **Incarnate Word**, who both creates and redeems, is **present to all**, having chosen to be so **before the foundation of the world**.

And therefore the Last Judgment will be one of **acceptance in the Beloved** (Jesus), not one of **condemnation**. Jesus will hand me to the Father and say, "Here's Robert; what do you think of him now?" And the Father will say, "Wonderful! Just what I had in mind for him all along!" And if at that point I want to say, "I don't like that" . . . well, then I can go to hell.

BUT NOT OTHERWISE.

(As I look at those notes, it occurs to me that I spent most of the time of the sermon dealing with the first three illustrations and with the final summary; I dealt with the points covered in the comments on specific verses much more briefly than the space given them above would indicate.) In any case, here's Dan.

❧   ❧

He walked up to me and started right in. "You did it again," he said: "harping on free grace and making the judgment of God sound as if it's some kind of picnic. Why do you always end up implying that being good or bad is a matter of indifference?"

I reached out and shook his hand. "I don't think that's quite what I said, Dan, but good morning, anyway. I suppose the quickest answer to your question is that I preach what I preach because I think the Gospels and the rest of the New Testament really say what I say — namely, that the only thing that saves us is forgiveness by the *grace of God.* Our *works* simply don't count in the ultimate balance: our good deeds can't get us a key to heaven, and our bad deeds can't get us locked out."

"Well, I doubt that. I believe in grace and forgiveness as much as anybody; but you take them way beyond bounds. What about the line in the Creed that says, 'He will come again in glory to judge the living and the dead'? Lately I've been looking at medieval paintings of the Last Judgment — and dipping into Dante as well for background. They show plenty of connection between what we do and our final state: those who are good go to heaven; those who are bad go to hell. According to what you say, that's all wrong; but according to them, whether someone's works are good or bad makes a big difference."

"Medieval paintings are not the New Testament, Dan. And neither is Dante. All I know is that both the Gospels and the Epistles make it quite clear that works *don't* count. Look at Jesus' parable of the Prodigal Son: the boy is forgiven *before* he makes

74

his confession to the father — while he's still, for all the father knows, a bum. And look at the parable of the Laborers in the Vineyard: those who did hardly anything are rewarded equally with the really good workers."

"That's all very well; but who else says the parables mean what you say they do?"

"Well, Paul, for one . . ."

"Paul is crazy."

"Maybe. Maybe not. But the Holy Spirit did at least manage to get him into the Bible. Look at the Epistle to the Romans, in chapter three: 'By the works of the law' — and those were all *good* works — 'no flesh will be justified.' Or how about Ephesians (which either Paul or somebody equally crazy wrote): 'For by grace you have been saved through faith, and this is not your own doing; it is the gift of God — not the result of works.'

"That's just Paul being crazy. Do you mean to tell me that there aren't passages in the Bible — maybe even in Paul — that say the exact opposite of what you say: that say in no uncertain terms that evil deeds will be punished?"

"Of course there are such passages. But the Bible is a big book, Dan. It's inspired by the Holy Spirit, sure. But that inspiration was at work through a lot of different ages and in a lot of different people — people who not only disagreed with one another but who sometimes disagreed with themselves when they got into different moods or had to address different situations. Given such a freewheeling process of inspiration, it's inevitable that the Bible is going to talk out of both sides of its mouth. You just have to decide which side of the mouth the Holy Spirit finally came down on. In other words, when you come across two passages that contradict each other, you have to decide which one you think the Holy Spirit really had in mind — and then you have to put the arm on the less central passage in favor of the more central one. All I can tell you is that for me, a passage like the one I quoted at the end of the sermon — Romans 8:1: 'There is therefore now

75

no condemnation for those who are in Christ Jesus' — comes very high on the list of central passages.'"

"But that only says there's no condemnation for those who are in Jesus. How can bad people pass a test like that? They're not in Jesus; they've turned their backs on him."

"Ah, but *Jesus* is in bad people. And Jesus hasn't turned his back on *them*. Don't you see? Jesus is all that counts. After all, he's the *Word of God* who made them, and he's the *Incarnate Word* who reconciles them. No matter what you or I may do or not do in our lives, the Gospel truth is that when we're dead, he's going to raise us, good or bad. And when he raises us, he's going to raise us *repaired*, not left in the mess of our sins. Of course, if you want to be like the guy in the parable of the King's Son's Wedding and refuse to put on the free tuxedo, then you can go to hell. But as I said, *not otherwise.*"

"Well, you should stop saying that. I've been in churches all over the world, and *nobody* says what you say. As far as I can see, even the church is against you. You're all alone."

"I don't think so, Dan. True enough, the church has peddled judgment as reward and punishment more often than it has reconciliation by grace. But not when it was at its best: in addition to Jesus and Paul, I've got the Reformers on my side. I'm not as lonely as you think. You may have a bit more company than I have; but it always puzzles me why your whole crowd is so fond of bad news. The Gospel is supposed to be about the Good News of salvation by grace, not about something you have to earn by getting your act together. Why does it bother you guys so much when somebody tells you God is going to take you all home for free?"

"Because there's no such thing as a free lunch, and because nobody but you says there is. Why do you insist on keeping it up? Why won't you just quit?"

Dan started walking toward the door, but I kept talking to him: "Well, I suppose one of the reasons I won't quit is that I

76

happen to like it. It's a *hoot,* Dan — the only honest-to-God free lunch the world has ever been offered. But more important than that, the Bible doesn't allow me to quit. And therefore I *can't* quit, no matter how many people think I'm reading Scripture wrong. The best I can give you is Luther's reply to his critics: *'Hie' steh' ich; ich kann nicht anders'* — 'Here I stand; I can do no other.'

He marched out, shaking his head. "You're impossible," he said. "Simply impossible."

SIX

The Mystery and the Incarnation

LOUISE: Well! He certainly got himself worked up, didn't he? Do people often get that angry at your sermons?

ROBERT: Not too often. But then, maybe preachers only hear from the more aggressive types; I'm pretty sure Dan was right when he claimed lots of other people shared his views. I'd even go so far as to say they're the silent majority of the church. Most of them will smile at least a little while you're up there preaching free grace and acceptance for everybody because it really does sound like Good News. But if you give them twenty minutes more to think about it — and to realize it let's in the riffraff of the world as well as them — it stops sounding so good to them. And once they've figured out it means God has forgiven even Hitler, they begin to think about tarring and feathering the messenger who brought them such outrageous news. It's one of the occupational hazards of the preaching trade. Jesus annoyed the hell out of quite a few of his listeners.

FRANK: Still, I think Dan had a point. You make it all sound so easy and light that people are going to get the idea they don't have to make any response at all to grace. Haven't you ever considered that maybe you're preaching what Bonhoeffer called "cheap grace" — that maybe you're actually missing the meaning of the judgment passages in the Bible? Don't works count at all? The Epistle of James says, "Faith, if it hath not works, is dead."

ROBERT: Frank, I never said there's no response to be made to grace — just that *faith* (trust) is the only possible response. It's the only response, in fact, that Jesus and Paul insist on. And what's more, neither one of them is about to allow you to turn faith into a *work* — not even if Bonhoeffer flirted with just that mistake (which I think he did). I think he was having an off day when he came up with the phrase "cheap grace." Grace can't be cheap, Frank: it's *free*. All you have to do is *believe* it — nothing else. I happen to think Jesus meant it when he said his yoke is easy and his burden light: when his audience asked him what they should do to work the works of God, he said, "This is the work of God, that you *believe* in the one whom he sent." He even went so far as to say, "God did not send the Son into the world to judge the world, but in order that the world might be saved through him. Those who believe in him are not judged." God simply doesn't count our works; he only asks us to *trust* the work he's done for us in Jesus.

FRANK: I still think you're giving us a fast shuffle. I want to hear you say something serious about judgment.

ROBERT: You will, Frank, you will. But not before I've set the subject in what I think is its serious New Testament context. Bear with me for a bit; I promise I'll give you plenty on judgment before I'm through.

For openers, the first thing I want to do is nail down a tight connection between the Mystery of Christ and the Incarnation. If you recall, I preached the sermon Dan objected to during the Christmas season; and I gave it the title *The Incarnation as the Gift of Universal Acceptance in Christ.* That's important here, because there are two very different ways you can come at the Incarnation. One is to turn it into a *transaction* that was poked into the history of the world at a specific time and place (namely, in the Person and work of Jesus); the other is to model it as a *feature of the constitution of the universe* — a Mystery present in creation from *beginning to end,* but which was finally and fully *manifested* to us in Jesus.

Let's talk about the transactional view first. Maybe the best way to show what's wrong with it as a model of the Incarnation is to work it up in terms of a football game. Look at what you get if you do that. Since you believe as a Christian that the God of the Old Testament is none other than the Holy Trinity — Father, Son, and Holy Spirit — but since the Incarnation as such is not mentioned in the Old Testament, you start out by saying that God the Father is the only Person of the Trinity involved in the game of history during the first half. God the Son, the Person who became incarnate in Jesus, simply wasn't on the field at all. Not only that, but the Father is involved principally as a coach, sending in players and plays from the heavenly sidelines. Still, even at that distance, he runs up an impressive if not decisive score: from the coin toss in Genesis 1 until just before the Angel Gabriel appears to Mary, he has things pretty well under control.

But then, during halftime, he decides to try a new strategy: he decides it's time to get Deity itself into the game. So, without ceasing to be the coach, the Father sends the Second Person of the Trinity — the Word who is God — into the game as a new quarterback who will be both divine and human at the same time. In other words, God becomes present in the game in a way he previously hadn't been. This works like a charm, of course: the third quarter of the game is an absolute rout. The opposition, while

80

it's not knocked out of the game completely, is so heavily scored against that for all practical purposes it hasn't got the chances of a snowball in a stewpot. But then, at the beginning of the fourth quarter, God the Father decides on the final, winning strategy. He pulls the divine-human quarterback out of the game (at the ascension of Christ), and he sends in God the Holy Spirit (at Pentecost) to empower and inspire his team all the way up to the final tick of the clock.

Now then. There are two things that are halfway decent about this football game model: it does correspond nicely to the progressive, "in-the-course-of-history" way that God actually revealed the Incarnation to the world; and it does give you not only a rousing victory at the end of the game but also the impression that the victory was in the bag from the start, since God (as one or another of the Persons of the Trinity) was involved in it all along.

But from the New Testament point of view, the model turns out to be a Model T — a heap. Because the New Testament says in a number of places that the Mystery of Christ — which is nothing other than the Incarnation of God in history — was active in the game from start to finish, not just in the third quarter (or in the third and fourth, if you say the Holy Spirit somehow managed to make the "ascended" quarterback present during the last fifteen minutes of the game).

For just a single instance of that New Testament view, look at the text for the sermon Dan got himself all worked up about. Ephesians 1:4 says that God *"chose us in Christ before the foundation of the world"* — before the game even started. In other words, there was never a time in all of history, or even prior to history, that every player in the game wasn't *"in Christ."* For two simple reasons: first, every player was present in and to the creating Word of God from all eternity; and second, the Word of God who was incarnate in Christ was present in and to every player by the Mystery of that Incarnation.

That means not only that the triumphant outcome of the

game of history was never in doubt, but that *everyone* was chosen to enjoy it. It means, in short, that the victory at the end was fully present to everyone from the beginning. This is why, incidentally, you can't expound the Good News of the Incarnation without doing at least some justice to the ideas of *election* (choosing) by God and *destination* (or predestination) by God. Those ideas alone get across the truth that it is God's efforts alone that win the game, not the players' efforts to obey the divine coach or the divine quarterback. The doctrine of Election reminds you that the *works* of the players in history are not the key to the success of history under God. And the doctrine of Predestination (provided you stay a million miles away from the idea that God predestines some people to damnation) guarantees that it's *his grace* and not *our merit* that's the effective, operative ingredient in the game.

Accordingly, it's time to junk the transactional, football-game model and hunt for a better one — one that will do justice to the Incarnation as a fact of the universe from the beginning rather than as a patch job tucked in as an afterthought at some point halfway through history. That's why, in my sermon, I suggested three further models of how the Incarnation "gets to us" (the Yearbook, the Ticket Window, and the Stadium open to all for free). But that's also why I eventually threw out the first two and settled on the last one.

Look for a minute at what's wrong with the Yearbook model: it falls flat on its axles in the garage and doesn't deliver the Incarnation to us at all. All it delivers is *our own remembrance* of the Incarnation — which is no more a real presence of the Word incarnate in Jesus than my remembrance of John F. Kennedy is a real presence of John F. Kennedy. More than that, its insistence on human remembering as the operative device leaves me strictly on my own as far as getting a grip on the work of Jesus is concerned. It does not say (as the New Testament does) that Jesus has already done a terrific job on me; the most it can say is that if I get myself sufficiently inspired by the memory of Jesus, I may be able to do a terrific job on myself. Which, if it is not an outright lie (mere remembrance of good examples has never yet succeeded as a way of getting the world's mess straightened up), is at least one of the most sweeping overstatements of all time. (If remembrance works at all, it works only for some people in some instances: most of us, most of the time, go right on being messes.)

Next, look at the Ticket Window model (with its casting of Jesus as the Official Ticket Seller). It starts off well enough: at least it says that the Incarnation is actually present somewhere — that Jesus is really there for the customers who show up at the window, and that once they've bought tickets from him, their presence in the Stadium is a sure thing. But then it begins to develop trans-actional engine trouble. First, it says that *only* those who show up at the window actually get tickets (thus deep-sixing Jesus' promise: "I, if I be lifted up from the earth, *will draw all to me*" — John 12:32). But second, it says that even showing up at the window doesn't guarantee them a ticket: they have to *buy* one, either with the hard cash of good works or with some kind of credit card that theologians might rig up for them (maybe by saying that God, when he comes across people with an invincibly ignorant lack of good works, just extends their credit limit — or decides he'll take American Express after all). But that's all hopeless. The cash-in-hand version violates the New Testament principle of salvation *gratis* — of our seat in the Stadium as a *free gift* that needs only to be *believed*, not *earned*. And the credit-card version substitutes a lot of computer fiction for the truth that God actually makes us good (righteous) in Jesus. Listen to Paul on the subject, in Romans 3:21-26 (italics mine):

> But now, apart from law, the *righteousness* of God has been disclosed, and is attested by the law and the prophets, the *righteousness* of God through *faith* in Jesus Christ for all who *believe*. For there is no distinction, since *all have sinned* and fall short of the glory of God; they are now justified by his grace *as a gift*,

through the redemption that is *in Christ Jesus,* whom God put forward as a sacrifice of atonement by his blood, effective through *faith.* He did this to show his righteousness, because in his divine forbearance he had *passed over the sins previously committed;* it was to prove at the present time that he himself is *righteous* and that he *justifies* the one who has *faith* in Jesus.

Therefore, it's only the last model — that of the Stadium open to all for free, free for nothing, filled with literally everybody in all of history — that does justice to the Mystery of the Incarnation. It says that we don't have to remember Jesus or even think about Jesus in order for the job done by the Word of God in Christ to be effective in us. And it says the job really is done. It makes it clear, in short, that we're all at the game already, complete with free beer, banners, and hot dogs — and that we've been there *from before the foundation of the world.* And therefore it says not only that we don't need to have the wherewithal (good works) for a ticket but that even to think we *could* buy a ticket is to misunderstand the whole setup. Furthermore, it says plainly that the only appropriate thing to do about such a fantastic arrangement is just shut up, believe it, and enjoy it — because we've already got it. And finally, it says that the only judgment issued in the whole process is one of *approval* and *inclusion,* not one of condemnation. If, of course, we choose to sit there in the Stadium and *not believe* we're there — if we want to believe we're condemned, when all the while "there is therefore now no condemnation" — we're free to do so. But all that will do for us is ruin our own enjoyment of the game — or possibly, if we take Jesus' parables of judgment seriously, get us kicked out of the Stadium altogether. But that's another subject, commonly called hell. For the moment, why don't you tell me what you think of all this so far?

FRANK: I think I see something of what you're trying to get at. But it still bothers me: what about Jesus' parables of judgment? Take the parable of the Talents, or the parable of the Wise and the Foolish Virgins. Don't they show that the judgment in the parables really was based on what the various characters did? The fellow who did nothing with the one talent he received is condemned; the ones who made more talents with their gift are praised. The wise virgins took the trouble to bring oil with their lamps; the foolish ones didn't. Doesn't that sound an awful lot like rewarding good works and damning bad ones?

ENID: Frankly — no pun intended, Frank — I wish we could get off all this bookkeeping about works and get on with the mystery of it all. Last year, when we read Julian of Norwich and Meister Eckhardt, I think we were a lot closer to the truth. They had no problem talking about the Incarnation as the "Incarnation of Christ in the *soul*," not just in Jesus or in Christians. It seems to me, Robert, that besides denying certain passages in the New Testament, these "commercial" views of the Incarnation sound suspiciously like Christian chauvinism. Your view of the Incarnation as already a fact for everyone at least allows room for the possibility that the other religions of the world have some legitimacy in and of themselves — that they're actually a picking up, albeit perhaps unconsciously, of an incarnation that's already present to everyone.

ROBERT: That's good, Enid; very good. I think you've hit on one of the most interesting consequences of what I would call the "catholicity" of the Incarnation: the heathen are not sitting out there in the dark waiting for us to bring them the light of Christ. They've already got it by the presence of the Incarnate Word. We can, of course, bring them the Good News of that presence as we've learned about it from Jesus. But in the process of doing that, it certainly wouldn't hurt if we took a look at the religions they presently have to see if they haven't, as you say, "picked up on it" somehow already. Lord knows, that was what Paul did with the Athenians, and what the Jesuits did in China till Rome shut them down, and what Thomas Merton was doing when he got electrocuted in a bathtub in India. But right now, I want to stick with Frank's problem . . .

OTTO: Well, I hope you won't stick with it too long. It seems to me we spend most of our time dealing with dumb Christian questions that don't even deserve answers. Jesus said he did what he did for everybody. People who are just itching to convert that into the bad news that he did it only for some should be given short shrift. Why, the way they talk, you'd think the Gospel was nothing more than an exercise in moral theology.

ROBERT: I agree with you a hundred percent, Otto. But since Christians are the only ones around to proclaim the Gospel, I think it's worth our time to try to persuade them not to proclaim it incorrectly. Let me get back to Frank, okay? Some of what I want to say will be familiar from my book called *The Parables of Judgment,* which we read a while ago; but some of it is new since then. Hang on: eventually I'll have some more shots of my own to take at moral theology.

OTTO: All right. But you owe me. Now you have two scorekeepers keeping an eye on you instead of just one.

ROBERT: You have my I.O.U. But then, so does Frank. Let me do the parable of the Talents for both of you.

The parable is obviously about judgment, but first let's get straight what the Greek word for judgment is: it's *krisis* — the same word as "crisis" in English. And it means the same thing: an act or situation that, because it puts a new set of rules into the game, calls for a new decision about the game on our part. It does not, in the first instance, mean "judgment" in the sense of *condemnation* (Greek has a number of other words for that). Because if you read Jesus' parables of judgment carefully, you'll see that the *krisis* in them — the primary judgment of God that calls us to a decision — always comes at the *beginning* of those parables. Furthermore, it's always a *krisis* caused by God's *favorable* judgment about us: he starts out each of those parables with a declaration that every one of the characters who stand for humanity is okay. It's a *krisis,* in other words, that Jesus sets up by having the "God" character declare at the outset that he's going to act on the basis of *the presumption — the effective declaration — of innocence.* It's a *krisis* of *faith,* therefore: none of the "human" characters has to prove he's *not* guilty by doing something to establish his innocence; the only thing any of them needs to do is *believe* in the innocence already proclaimed over him.

Look at a few instances. The guests invited to the king's son's wedding are all judged equally worthy of being at a royal wedding. All ten virgins are members of the bridal party. And all three servants, whether they receive five talents, or two, or one, are equally in their master's favor. They all receive a judgment of *acceptability,* of *inclusion.* They're all *presumed innocent.* Nobody is condemned to start with.

Now, obviously, at the ends of those parables, there's plenty of condemnation. But it's crucial to note what that condemnation is based on. The temptation, of course (since we're totally committed to justifying ourselves by our own goodness), is to read the hard-hearted endings as based on evil works — on the characters' failure to *perform properly.* But that just won't wash. What the final judgment is really based on is not their works but the presence or absence of *their faith* in the God-character who graciously included them in his favor from square one.

So let's look at the parable of the Talents (Matt. 25:14-30) in that light. A businessman is going away on a trip. He calls his three top employees together and gives each of them a fantastic amount of money. (A talent was a lifetime's earnings for a working person, so even the fellow who got one talent got a bundle.) And the businessman expects his employees to do only one thing with the money: they are (to borrow a phrase from the corresponding parable in Luke) to "do business" — that is, to act *in faith to him,* to act as his *fiduciaries.* The *krisis,* therefore, is one of *inclusion* in the businessman's favor.

The first two respond properly to that *krisis.* The one with five talents hustles and makes five more with them; the one with two, two more. But the third employee doesn't do business with his one talent at all. Instead, he digs a hole in the ground and hides the money for safekeeping.

Now here's where you have to start reading carefully. When the businessman returns, he wants to see what his employees have done with the talents — to look at their accounts and see what kind of fiduciaries they've been. Well, you know the story. With the first two, he's completely satisfied that they've acted in faith to his interests. He says to each of them, "Well done, good and *faithful* servant" — and he gives them even more of his trust, setting them over "many things" and inviting them into a joyful, personal relationship with himself.

LOUISE: But he says "*good* and faithful," not just "faithful." Doesn't that mean we have to be *both?*

Thank you, Louise: it's always nice to have you around, listening to every word. Okay then, here's something on the phrase "good and faithful." The fact that the word "good" is put in first place tends to make people read it as the most important word in the businessman's mind — as if he's telling his employees they've been first of all good, and then (more or less incidentally) faithful.

But I don't read it that way. "Good and faithful," for me, is just another way of saying "perfectly faithful" — just as "good and hot" or "good and tired" are other ways of saying "perfectly heated" or "completely ready for bed." In other words, "good" here is not an adjective used in the normal way to modify "servant," but an adjective used adverbially to modify "faithful." And that fits in nicely with the *krisis of faith* — the *krisis* of the invitation to the employees to *trust* the businessman's inclusion of them at the beginning of the parable. In the final reckoning, he looks principally at the *faithfulness* that their gung-ho hustling attests to, not at the incidental results of that hustling.

But back to the rest of the parable. Finally, the third employee comes in and goes through a song and dance about how he knows the businessman is a greedy monster who will do even crooked deals if they'll make him a buck — and how, therefore, he was so afraid to lose even a penny of the money that he hid it in the ground. "See," he says, handing the talent back; "here's what's yours — every cent of it."

Time to read carefully again. What the third employee gets, of course, is a blast of condemnation ("You wicked and lazy servant!") followed by a withering refutation of his reasons for hiding the money ("If you knew I drove such hard bargains, you could at least have put my money in a savings account and gotten me a lousy three and a half percent!").

Do you see the point? If all the businessman was interested in was the money itself, why wouldn't he just take back the talent and make a mental note not to waste his time on this bozo again? Why the anger? Why the uncharacteristic suggestion that maybe moneylenders' interest rates would be just as appealing to him as the hundred percent profit the other two employees made for him? Do you know why? It's because he wasn't primarily interested in the money at all; only in the *faithfulness* of the employees to his interests. I have a theory that if the fellow who received the five talents had come back and reported that he'd lost the whole five

89

on an incredible deal that went sour at the last minute, the businessman would have said to him, "Well, that's not so good; but at least you were good and faithful, and that's all that counts. Better luck to both of us next time." And if you still think the businessman in the parable is a stand-in for a God who's counting every penny, and whose main concern is settling scores on the basis of strict justice, what do you make of the fact that when he takes the one talent back from the piker who had it, he gives it to the fellow who already has ten? Why didn't he give it to the one who only had four? After all, that one made a hundred percent profit too, so he was just as good a business risk.

But enough, perhaps. The point of this tirade is that the parable is not about fairness, or justice, or rendering to people the due reward of their labors. It's about *faith*. And so are most of Jesus' other parables. They're full of details designed to make a moral theologian's flesh crawl. The wise virgins are rewarded for being a bunch of snot-noses, while the foolish ones are kicked out for something that was more the bridegroom's fault than theirs. The rotten prodigal is given more of a party than his Mr. Wonderful brother. The Johnny-come-lately workers in the vineyard are given a full day's pay for next to no work. Why such inequities? Why such big rewards for crummy types? I'll tell you why. It's because Jesus cares only about whether people are someplace where *trust alone* can get them, not about whether they can claim to have worked their way there by noble efforts. So in his stories he goes out of his way to reward those whose only virtue consists of trusting enough to be in the right place at the right time (like the tax collector in the parable of the Pharisee and the Publican) — and he usually gives them shabby reasons for being there, just to make sure you won't have any stray virtues to keep track of. And that's because the Gospel is not some self-improvement scheme devised by a God who holds back on us till he sees the improvements. Above all, Jesus wants to make sure we understand he doesn't care a fig about our precious results. It doesn't even make a difference to him if we're solid brass bastards, because "while we were still sinners, Christ died for the ungodly." By the Mystery of the Incarnation, he has included everybody, from Aalborg to Zzwickendorf. He's had you home free from the start, no matter what you've done; all you have to do is *believe* him. Therefore, God isn't *fair:* if he were fair, we'd all be in the soup. God is *good:* crazy, starkstaring-bonkers good.

OTTO: Well! That's more like it. You get your I.O.U. back marked "paid."

ROBERT: No, Otto; I insist on paying in full. I still owe Frank something on why faith *can't* be a work.

First, let's be sure we understand what a *work* is. A work is an operation designed, planned, and executed by someone in order to achieve an end or goal. If I'm going to make a hamburger for supper, I first have to have the design, the idea of a hamburger firmly in mind (ground beef, shaped into a patty, fried or broiled, served on a bun, with pickle, ketchup, relish, or mustard, and so on). Next, I have to make plans to implement that design (set a time to shop for meat and buns, choose between frying and broiling, decide whether to put the relish on the burger or on the table, and so forth). Finally, I must actually execute the design as planned (go to the store, shape the meat, cook it, set the table, and do whatever other actual labor is necessary). But note carefully that the work of producing a hamburger demands that I be able to master *every one of those steps.* If I don't have a clue as to what a hamburger is, I'm dead from the start. If I'm not capable of making sensible and adequate plans to produce one, I'm out of luck. And if I'm unwilling or unable to do the culinary dog-work involved, I won't have a hamburger for supper. In other words, without *total competence on my part,* I get no finished work.

Next, though, consider some things that are *not* works. Suppose I want to make an apple. The first thing I have to understand is that *I'm not able to make one:* only an apple tree can do that. So, instead, I plant some apple trees. That action, of course, is a work I'm capable of; and it gives me plenty of additional works to do because I'm also able to design, plan, and execute a program of apple-growing. Still, the apples I finally get will, strictly speaking, be the trees' work, not mine: my exertions in all three departments will be activities based on a *trust* that the apple trees will do the principal job. My works will indeed be my very own; but they will not be works that *make apples.* In short, they will be *acts of faith,* not works.

But to see the faith/works distinction more clearly, we have to take the illustration several steps further.

Suppose that I'm in the hospital — bedridden, blind, and broke — and that all my friends have been telling me that if I don't get my house painted, my siding is going to rot. And then suppose that one day you visit me and tell me that the painter you hired to do the outside of my house has just put the finishing touches on the whole job. You invite me, in other words, to *trust your word* and stop worrying about my siding. Now then: how does that act of faith (if I make it) rate as a *work?* The answer is, it doesn't. It didn't *design* the job you did for me. It involved no *plan* on my part to have the job done: I couldn't plan to do it myself because I was bedridden and blind; and I couldn't plan to hire somebody to do it because I was broke. And it didn't *execute* anything: even if I had had all the "faith" in the world before you told me the house was painted, I myself would still have had no power to do the job. Therefore, there is no part of the *work* of painting that I could have managed on my own. So the only thing left for me to do about the paint job you tell me of is either *disbelieve* you and go on being miserable about the condition of my house, or *believe* you, relax in gratitude, and enjoy the work you did for me.

It's this illustration, you see, that goes to the heart of the distinction between faith and works. Consider some questions. Is my faith in you a work, a string of effective actions that *caused* you to paint my house? No: the paint job was entirely your idea *prior to my faith,* and your doing it involved no cooperation whatsoever on my part. Is my faith then something that *led* you (out of pity, perhaps) to design, plan, and execute your project? No again: it never even occurred to me to trust you until you told me you had done the job totally on your own. (You may have done it out of pity or kindness, of course, but those were your own promptings, not responses to the leading of my faith.) Well then, is your paint job perhaps a *reward* for my faith? Again, no: your doing of it preceded my faith; it was finished and handed to me before I heard any word of it I could believe. My faith, therefore, *does nothing except enable me to enjoy your gift.* It is not, and it cannot be, a work. And, above all, it is not, and it cannot be, a condition of your work. Your work was simply a gift dropped in my lap like an apple — or, better said, like some weird, exotic fruit I never even thought of. All I can do is trust and taste, or disbelieve and go on feeling deprived.

But I want to follow up on that notion of the weird, exotic fruit — because it's the clincher that ties all this to the Gospel. People talk as if their "having faith" or their "working up enough faith" might actually cause the occurrence of things that would solve their problems. Well, let me point something out to you: the gift that the Gospel drops in our lap and invites us to believe is not a gift anybody in his right mind can think of as solving problems in that simple, causal sense. It's a weird and exotic gift that solves no present problems at all; and it's a gift that no one in the whole history of the world ever thought of, wanted, or prayed for. Who, for example, ever prayed a prayer like this: "Please, God, reward our faith in you by becoming incarnate in a failed Messiah who will then die, rise, and disappear, and subsequently claim to have made the whole creation new, while everybody's life goes right on being just as nasty, mean, brutish, and short as it was before"? The answer, of course, is nobody. Left to our own devices, we might pray for pie in the sky, or caviar on earth, or for anything else that would make us a spiritual or temporal buck — but never for this bizarre program of salvation *in our disasters* rather than *out of them.* It never even occurred to us to want such a thing; *yet that's precisely the scenario the Gospel invites us to believe in.* Not only that, but when we take a good, sensible look at it, it seems more like cruelty than kindness. Accordingly, the only possible response to such a gift is not a bunch of intelligible works that will ace God into giving us what we consider a helping hand. Rather, it's an absurd decision to trust an absurd Mystery — the Mystery of a God who is incarnate in an *otherwise unimproved world* — an invisible pig in a very grimy poke indeed.

Faith, therefore, is an absurdity answering an absurdity. And since no work gets anywhere unless it is *not absurd,* faith cannot be a work. Admittedly, faith always involves some kind of *activity* on our part: it's a decision to trust; and we make that decision with our ordinary, decision-making apparatus. Even when we hear God's promises, we hear them with ordinary human ears, we think about them with ordinary human brains, and we choose to trust them — or not to trust them — with ordinary human wills. Even if you hold that faith is a gift of God, it's still a gift given to human beings, not angels. Therefore, faith without activity on our part — "without works," as Frank reminded us by quoting from the Epistle of James — is indeed dead.

Nevertheless, while it's possible to talk about "the works of faith" that way, it's probably not a good idea to do so very often. The risk of confusing faith and works is simply too great. If I had my druthers, I'd prefer to talk about "activities of faith," or "faith in action," just to keep works from sabotaging the notion of faith. For the record then, here's a summary of the whole business:

Works are always *productions, operations, acts of making or doing:* they invariably call for *knowledge* on our part of what needs to be done and *capacity* on our part to do it. *Faith,* by contrast, is an activity of *trusting somebody else's knowledge and capacity* to accomplish something we couldn't manage — and, in the case of faith in the Mystery of the Incarnation, of *trusting God* to accomplish it *in a way that looks for all the world like doing nothing whatsoever.*

All right. What are your reactions to that?

FRANK: I must say I was surprised to hear you say something positive about the Epistle of James. I expected you to just take Luther's position and call it "an epistle of straw." But seriously, I'm beginning to see how easy it is to turn faith into a work — and how people who do that reduce the Gospel to nothing more than what they could have thought up themselves rather than honor it as something only God could have invented. I still wonder, though, about the passages in the parables that really do seem to reward good works. You think maybe Jesus wasn't as impressed by the faith/works distinction as Paul and you are? I'll grant you that your explanation of the parable of the Talents goes a long way to convince me it's really about faith. But what about the rest of Matthew 25: the parable of the Wise and the Foolish Virgins, and the parable of the Great Judgment, with its separation of the sheep and the goats?

ALICE: I'd like to hear you do something with those too. I can't recall ever having heard a sermon on the virgins in which the extra oil the wise ones brought with their lamps *wasn't* equated with good works.

ROBERT: Okay. Virgins first; then Sheep and Goats. I've already stressed the fact that the parable of the Ten Virgins begins with a *krisis of approval,* a judgment of acceptability. Any objections to that?

95

ENID: Not from me. Keep going.

FRANK: Me, either. I'll let you have inclusion before exclusion on that one.

ROBERT: Good. But how about my insistence that the wise virgins weren't nice girls?

ALICE: I've got no problems with that, either. I've always thought they were awful — and wondered why Jesus would hold up such terrible characters for admiration.

ROBERT: Right. So let me go to the heart of the matter, which is the decision of the foolish virgins to go shopping for oil at midnight instead of staying at the party in which they'd already been included. Why do you think they did that?

LOUISE: Well, I suppose it was because they somehow thought they wouldn't be acceptable to the bridegroom if their lamps weren't lit.

ROBERT: That's exactly right, Louise. *They* thought. *They* told themselves that fairy tale. They and they alone were the ones who dreamt up that requirement. And they dreamt it up precisely because they didn't *trust* the bridegroom. They imagined that there was some work they still had to do in order to be approved of by him, when all the while his approval of them was a sure thing from the start. All they had to do was stay put and trust it.

ENID: Yes. Worrying about not having lit lamps was no more relevant to their status as members of the wedding than worrying about a torn hem or a broken high heel would be. Those things happen at weddings; but sensible people don't let them spoil a good party. The foolish bridesmaids were just that: *fools*. And can we please get rid of the anachronism of calling them virgins? There probably hasn't been a virgin in a wedding party in this parish for years.

ROBERT: Thank you, Enid. The clergy don't keep statistics on that sort of thing, but we do sometimes wonder. "Bridesmaids" it is from here on out. But tell me something. Do you all agree with my insistence that when these five bridesmaids go traipsing all over town knocking on shop doors with "Closed" signs, they're substituting works for faith?

LOUISE: I suppose so. But what was so horrible about what they did? Maybe they were just trying to please the bridegroom. It's still hard for me to see why he was so severe with them. What else could they have done?

ROBERT: They could have used a little imagination, Louise — and maybe a little charm. Why couldn't they each have walked out to meet the bridegroom *alongside* one of the five who had a burning lamp? Who said each of them had to have a lit lamp of her very own? The two-girls-to-a-lamp approach would have been a charming effect, and one that wouldn't have violated the spirit of the party.

OTTO: Of course. Which is exactly what they did when they got back from their futile trip and raised a ruckus by banging on the door while the bridegroom's brother was singing "O, Promise Me."

ROBERT: You have the makings of a great expositor, Otto: imagination like that is what the parables cry out for. You've hit on the real reason the bridegroom was so angry at them: because they messed up the party — or, better said (because it's *his* party and they have no power at all to mess it up), because they denied the bridegroom's delight in having them at it. So the only thing they really messed up was their own happiness.

ENID: Yes. And the root of that happiness was waiting in trust for the bridegroom to come and actually enjoy their presence at his party. What Jesus is really saying to us in this parable is, "Wait for me. Stay at the party I've thrown for you even if *all* the lights go out and you're sitting in the dark. I'll find you even if you're lost, alone, decrepit, or dead. I'll *be* there. Just stay put in your trust and you'll see."

ROBERT: That's excellent, Enid; and it's borne out by what Jesus actually has the bridegroom say to the foolish bridesmaids when they try to re-include themselves after their untrusting self-exclusion. They knock on the door and plead with him: "Sir, Sir, open up for us." But he answers, "Truly, I tell you, I don't know you." Do you see the point? What he's really saying is, "You turkeys! You were already in and you walked out for some stupid reason of your own. I just don't understand party poopers like you at all." Seen in that light, the parable of the Ten Bridesmaids is simply a variant of the parable of the King's Son's Wedding. The idiot who wouldn't put on the free wedding costume was kicked out for the same reason the five foolish bridesmaids were: he was already included, but wouldn't act as if he believed it. Once again, the initial *krisis* is one of *favorable judgment;* and the final judgment is a condemnation only of those who won't respond to that *krisis* in faith. It's not a condemnation of their works on the basis of worthiness but a condemnation of the lack of faith manifested by their actions. "Faith without actions," therefore, is not only dead; it's nonexistent.

OTTO: All right. All right. But let's get on with it: Sheep and Goats, please.

ROBERT: That okay with you, Frank?

FRANK: Yes. That's not only the clearest condemnation passage but also the one I can't see you getting around.

ROBERT: I don't need to get around it, Frank. I actually think it says what I'm saying, if you read it carefully. But first you have to grant me that faith is not a gimmick we can use to ace somebody who's basically against us into being favorable to us. You have to grant me it's trust in a *relationship* with someone who's already accepted us. Okay?

FRANK: It always gives me the willies when you put in those "but firsts." I get the impression I'm being cut off at the knees but just haven't felt it yet.

ROBERT: All right, Frank. Let's take it step by step. The Lamb of God takes away the sins of the world, right? Are you still with me?

FRANK: Yes.

ROBERT: And when he takes them away, does he get them all, or does he miss some?

FRANK: All, I guess.

ROBERT: So that means God has solved all his problems with sin — with evil deeds, with wicked works, right? As far as he's concerned, he's in a favorable relationship with everyone, even the stinkers.

FRANK: That strikes me as going too fast.

ROBERT: Why? It's precisely what the parable of the Sheep and the

99

Goats — or the Judgment of the Nations, to give it a better name — actually says. First of all, it's about the response of the *nations* — the *Gentiles,* not the Jews — to the Good News of the Mystery of God's presence in the world. That means it's about a *catholic relationship,* a universal intimacy with the whole world. And it's about the *primacy,* the *sole, operative effectiveness* of that relationship. That's proved in the parable by the fact that neither the sheep nor the goats knew what they were doing when they ministered, or didn't minister, to the King as he was present in "the least of his brethren." Neither of them had a clue that they were doing any work at all, good or bad. The sheep just happened, by their ministering, to relate themselves to that presence; and the goats just happened, by their not ministering, to fail to relate themselves to it. It wasn't their works, therefore, that earned them the King's relationship with them, because that was a given; it was the absence of something that could count as trust in that given that got them in Dutch. And that's proved by the fact that if *he hadn't been present* in all those broken-down types the parable lists, it wouldn't have mattered beans how many good works they did or didn't do. *He,* not they, is the one who made the difference; it was *his presence* in all the broken of the world that was the *krisis* of approval he offered them. And therefore the main point of the parable is the point he goes out of his way to make twice: "Inasmuch as you did it [or didn't do it] to one of these 'least of my brethren,' you did it [or didn't do it] *to me.*" It's their *unknowing actions of faith in his presence* that "save" them, not their carefully figured-out works.

LOUISE: But how could the goats be condemned then? They weren't guilty of anything. They didn't know what they were doing, either.

ROBERT: That's a large subject, Louise; but the short answer to your question is that Latin moral theology hadn't been invented when Jesus told this parable. Because your question makes sense only in terms of the abstract logic-chopping of medieval moralists and their modern counterparts: the kind of reasoning that gets your case dismissed if you can prove you didn't know what you were doing. Fortunately, though, Jesus wasn't the least bit interested in such stuff. He was concerned only to put himself — in his saving, absolving, accepting relationship with the world — in the center of the picture. He was trying to tell us (to say it again for about the hundredth time today) that there's a party already going on despite our works, and that if we will only trust it, we'll realize we're already okay. True enough, he does ring the chimes on "everlasting fire reserved for the devil and his angels," and "everlasting punishment" — but only because that's the way a rabbi of his time would tell such a story. Back then, they weren't the least afraid to put in a bit of mayhem to underscore their points. But no matter how severe it may sound to us, it's still not a bad description of what it's like to talk yourself out of the last party in town. The point of both this parable and the parable of the Ten Bridesmaids is that if, for whatever reasons, you don't choose to be in the terrific place he's put you, you're just plain out of decent places to be. He's not into moral theology, he's into party theology. He's not talking about works that can be rewarded or punished; he's talking about faith in something already in full swing.

FRANK: Okay. So let that pass. But what do you have to say to the passages that talk about "*repent* and believe"? Don't they imply that there's still something to do in addition to believing? And what about "works worthy of repentance"? Doesn't that mean that works count?

ROBERT: No. And for a couple of reasons. First of all, "repent" is a translation of the Greek *metanoein,* which means "change your mind," or "turn your mind around." And therefore I wouldn't read "repent and believe" the way you just did — as if it meant "repent first, and then, when you've got that job done right, believe." I'd read it as a double imperative doing duty for a conditional statement of a single truth: sort of like "Spare the rod and spoil the child," which really means "If you spare the rod, you will inexorably spoil the child." If you read "repent and believe" that way, it turns out to mean "If you get your mind turned around from not believing, you will inexorably be led to believe." And therefore "repent and believe" refers to a single act by which we go from unfaith to faith. Repentance is simply part of the process of believing; it's not some separate work that earns us brownie points apart from believing.

Second, the phrase "works worthy of repentance" occurs only once in the New Testament — when Paul was explaining his conversion and his preaching to Agrippa in the twenty-sixth chapter of Acts. He said: "Therefore, King Agrippa, I was not disobedient to the heavenly vision, but declared first to those in Damascus, then to those in Jerusalem and throughout the countryside of Judaea, and also to the Gentiles that they should repent and turn to God, doing works worthy of repentance." But since what he was really declaring to all those possible converts was not some program of ethical improvement but the death and resurrection of Jesus as the Light to both Jews and Gentiles, the only thing he can reasonably be taken to mean as "works worthy of repentance" is "actions declaratory of belief rather than unbelief" in that Light — actions befitting the turnaround from unfaith to faith.

The same thing is true of John the Baptist, though it's worth noting that he didn't use the word "works": he told his hearers to "bear *fruit* worthy of repentance." Now, no matter what John himself may have had in mind, if you're going to work up a theology of repentance out of that phrase, you have to take into account what the Holy Spirit did with it later on when he got Paul to make the crucial distinction between "the works of the flesh" and "the fruit of the Spirit." Works are things you do in one department to get results in another: I do my cooking in the chef department, for example, but the results exist in another department — namely, on the table. In the case of a fruit, however, the result is in the same department (namely, the tree) from start to finish. Once again, therefore, you've got repentance and faith as two actions within the single category of *believing*.

But this has been a long session. Why don't we give Frank one last shot, if he'd like, and call it a day?

FRANK: Well, all right. But since you've at least slowed me down a little in my objections, let me ask a question that I think was behind what Dan was upset about at the church door. If you say that the acceptance is already given freely to everybody in the world by the Mystery of the Incarnation — and that all anyone has to do is believe it — what's the incentive for living a good life as opposed to a rotten one? What, for that matter, is the incentive for believing as opposed to not believing?

ROBERT: Ah! The real question at last — the one all of us have, whether we ask it or not. Okay. Here's my answer: the incentive is that the Gospel is *fun*. As I said to Dan, it's a *hoot*: it's the only really good news the world will ever hear. It may be mysterious, or absurd, or outrageous; but it will make you gladder than anything the world will ever tell you. As a matter of fact, all the world will ever give you is a lifetime's supply of threatening incentives to get your act together, or else.

People always assume that the church's primary business

103

is to teach morality. But it isn't; it's to proclaim grace, for-giveness, and the free party for all. It's to announce the rec-onciling relationship of God to everybody and to invite them simply to believe it and celebrate it. Morality, law, rules, prescriptions — those are all the world's business. And the world keeps up a steady drumbeat on those subjects: you must do this; you mustn't do that; you're out until you can prove yourself worthy of being let in. But that's just a thinly dis-guised way of saying that most people aren't going to be in for very long and that none of them can be in for good. Nobody, from Adam to the last person on earth, can pass a test like that. And therefore God simply doesn't risk it: by the Mystery of the Incarnation, he cancels all the tests and gives a blanket hundred percent to everyone. In the Mystery of Christ's death, he drops all the rotten works in the world down the black hole of his own forgetting; and in the Mystery of Christ's resurrection, he makes a new world in which we're all home free.

And if that's not incentive enough for anybody, I'm afraid I'm out of incentives. All I can say is, I agree with the bridegroom: "I just don't understand party poopers like that at all."

FRANK: Can I say one last thing? You're not going to believe this, but suddenly I just got it! You've all been saying it one way or another every time you referred to the nastiness of the wise virgins, but it wasn't until just now that it sank in: *the key to the parables is the badness of the good characters!* Every time Jesus wants to make sure that the point of his story will be faith and not works, or grace and not merit, he presents the characters who get rewarded as unreformed crumb buns. And just to make sure you won't think he's talking about punishing evil works, he tells his stories in such a way that *it's the very goodness of the bad characters that gets in the way of their acting in faith.* That's why the parables always seem so upside down. The prodigal, who gets the welcome-home party, is a scoundrel; his elder brother, who's having a miserable time out in the yard, is Mr. Right. The publican, who gets justified, just stands in the temple and says he's no good; the Pharisee, who gets condemned, is a good person. The laborers who get a whole day's pay for only an hour's work are a bunch of freeloaders; the all-day laborers who get chewed out are responsible workers. And as you said, the wise virgins can only be seen as incomprehensibly snotty, while the foolish ones can be given all kinds of good excuses for trying to do what they think is right. In all those parables, the only thing that good works seem to be good for is keeping people from acting in faith. So it's faith, not works, that's the real point of the parables. There! Are you with *me* now?

ROBERT: Well! I should think so! One never knows, does one?

OTTO: One never does. I might even apologize for trying to rush things.

ALICE: I think this calls for something special. Why don't we sing the Doxology?

OTTO: Fine. As long as it's pitched lower than we sing it in church.

ROBERT: Well, it's usually in G, but I think I can manage to start it in F.

ENID: Wonderful! F for faith as opposed to G for good works.

LOUISE: Or F for free.

FRANK: Or F for fun — in four parts, if we can manage it.

ROBERT: All right, then. Let's do it:

> Praise God, from whom all blessings flow;
> Praise him, all creatures here below;
> Praise him above, ye heavenly host:
> Praise Father, Son, and Holy Ghost. Amen.

SEVEN

Mabel

When I introduced Dan to you back in Chapter Five, I walked you across a rather forbidding front porch: an explanation of how I preach, a full biblical text, and a possibly mystifying expansion of the notes I used for the sermon that bothered him. This time around, I shall be brief to a fault.

Mabel Perkins was sixtyish. I'd never met her before, and to the best of my knowledge she had never attended the parish church. I had a total of three sessions with her, but I've compressed them into two here (without, I think, losing anything important in the original encounters). Anything else you need to know will come out in the conversation that follows.

The First Session

She was a good twenty minutes late when she arrived at my office just after 10:50 A.M. "Father Capon?" she asked as she appeared in the open doorway. "I'm sorry I'm late, but I just couldn't get off the phone this morning. And then it took me a while to find the right driveway into the church parking lot. If you have to do something else now, just tell me and I'll come again another time."

I stood up to greet her. "No, no, Mabel. It's perfectly all right. That driveway isn't the world's best-marked entrance. Newcomers almost always miss it. Have a seat — and since I've already used your first name, why don't you just call me Robert?"

I motioned her to one of the two comfortable armchairs opposite my desk and sat myself down in the other. "So. What can I do for you?"

"I'm having difficulty dealing with the death of my husband," she said. "I just seem unable to stop thinking about it and bursting into tears over it. My friend Marta, who's been staying with me, thought it might be a good idea if I talked with someone who deals with death frequently, and she suggested you. So here I am. In all honesty, though, I can't think of a thing you might say that would help. It's just grief, I suppose — and I'm expecting the grieving process to go faster than it does."

"At this point," I said, "I can't think of what I might say, either. Why don't you fill me in a bit: how long ago he died; whether it was suddenly or after a long illness; how old he was; and anything else you care to tell me about your life with him. Were you married long?"

"Nineteen years. We were married back in 1972; it was a second marriage for both of us. We met when he was a professor of history at the University of Michigan in Ann Arbor and I was in the psychology department. (I was doing some teaching at the time, but I was mostly involved in setting up psychological testing programs.) He was a brilliant historian. After he retired, we stayed around in Ann Arbor for a few years. But you know how those things are. Once you're out of the academic loop, things aren't the same. Colleagues you thought were friends gradually turn out to have been only colleagues. So in '87, we came here and found a small place that was just right for us. Actually, my friends found it for us, but we loved it the minute we saw it, and we've been here ever since."

She started to fill up and reached for a tissue to dry her eyes.

"There! You see how it is. All I have to do is make some little slip like that — saying 'we' when it's just me now — and it all comes over me again."

"I know. Just keep going when you're ready."

"I'm sorry about that," she said. "Where was I?"

"Your friends found the house for you. Was your husband in good health?"

"Oh, yes. He was in wonderful health for a man of seventy-four — right up to just before he died. He'd slowed down a bit, of course, but he was just as sharp mentally as he'd ever been. It was so sudden — such a waste."

I waited for her to dry her eyes again. "You know," I said, "people always assume that a sudden death is somehow preferable to a lingering one. But if you've been close to someone for — what, nineteen years? — no death is the only thing that's really preferable. You can't see the tissue of two decades of living together torn to pieces and not be affected by it."

"But that's the odd part of it. We were apart a good deal. And even when we were together, we had our separate interests. I'm involved in a number of professional associations, and the meetings took me away quite frequently. But he kept right on with his reading and writing. He was a very self-contained person. So we simply didn't live on top of each other all the time. That's why I'm so surprised by these outbursts. I'd have thought I could make a better adjustment."

Again, I waited; then I asked her, "How did he die?"

"Ah, that!" she said suddenly. "It was four months ago. I was away at a conference in Philadelphia — nothing unusual, as I said — and he was at home as he always was. Then one evening Marta called me and said he'd been taken to the hospital with chest pains and that they'd put him in the coronary care unit. So I called his doctor, and when I finally got through, he told me that it seemed to be a minor episode and that after some further tests, they'd probably send him home. Then I called Fred, and I got the same story from him; he sounded good, and he said that the pains were gone. I told him that if he wanted me to, I'd come right back up to be there with him. But he was very much against that. He didn't like even a hint of talk about death, and he wasn't any kind of believer at all. So I stayed on at the conference and just called him every day. When the conference was over, though, a friend of mine asked me to visit her for a few days, so I asked him again whether I should come home. He still sounded fine (he was in a regular room by then), and he still insisted I didn't need to, so I went ahead and stayed in Philadelphia — leaving my friend's phone number with the hospital and the doctor, just in case they had to get in touch with me.

"But then, the second night I was at my friend's house, the phone call came from Marta saying he'd died of a massive coronary. I called the doctor and the hospital immediately and tried to get somebody to tell me what had happened, but they were both uncommunicative, to say the least. The doctor said something like, 'These things are always unpredictable, especially at his age,' and the hospital practically said nothing except that I should talk to the doctor. I came right home the next morning, and to this day, no matter how hard I've tried, I've never gotten a scrap more information from anybody. Doesn't that sound strange to you? It's almost as if they're afraid to talk to me — as if some kind of cover-up is going on."

I hesitated for a moment. "It seems to me we've got two subjects here, maybe even three. May I be frank?"

"I suppose so. Yes."

"Well, the first is grief. The second is indignation at the thought of possible negligence . . ."

She broke in. "But doesn't it seem to you like negligence?"

"I don't know," I said. "First of all, I simply haven't heard any hard evidence of it — and at least at this point in our conversation, it seems to me that you haven't, either. You could be right, of course: such things happen. But you could be wrong. Or you could be right and never be able to prove it."

110

She started to interrupt, but I went right on. "Hear me out, if you can. Whatever the case may be, let's lay the negligence business aside for a moment. The third thing that may be going on is guilt on your own part at not having come back up here when your husband was in the hospital — at not having been here when he died. I'm not saying that medical negligence or the feeling of guilt on your part couldn't be real problems — but your grief certainly is. So I want to talk about those two only after we've had a chance to think a bit about the grief. Okay?"

"All right. But . . ."

She stopped herself; I continued. "Look. You're the psychologist here. You probably know more about grief as a subject than I do. You may even have had more personal experience with it, for all I know. But in either case, you know that grieving is a natural process that takes time to run its course. There are stages you simply have to slop through. The funeral, at least as we run them in this country now, isn't really part of the process. Unless you're from a Mediterranean background and feel free to wail, scream, and fall on the coffin all you like, you expect yourself to be more or less in control of your emotions. And that, plus all the arrangements and all the company, simply delays the beginning of the process till you're all alone. Which is a tough time to begin, because besides the death, you then have to face the shipwreck of your previous life. How long that lasts depends on a lot of things: your own resilience; your gentleness and patience with yourself over your own collapsing; and your firm resolve, deep down somewhere, to let the process run its course while you get on with your life as it now is and can be. You can't do much to speed it up. After a couple of months, your daily life may be a little easier — even brighter. But then along comes a birthday, or an anniversary, or a vacation period, or a holiday like Christmas or Thanksgiving, and its Collapse City all over again. To get through even the worst of it may take a year or more — and even after that, any poignant memory can find you a sitting duck.

"But — and this is the important thing — *you mustn't try to get through it all by distracting yourself from your loss*. That only keeps you from living where you really are. Instead, you must try gently but firmly to reinstall your good memories of the person who died in the life you now have. You even have to try to reinstall your bad memories, if any, by facing them and giving absolution to all concerned — even, and especially, to yourself. Anything else would be a denial of your history. And that, as you know, is always a bad idea. Therefore, whatever helps you reinstall that history in your new present is a good idea; and whatever keeps you from facing it as it really was is something you have to watch out for. Do you agree with that?"

"Yes," she said. "I've read the books too. But it just doesn't seem to help. Isn't there something you can tell me that will?"

"Maybe. Let's see. A minute ago, I said you mustn't try to get through the grief by distracting yourself from your loss. I want to add something to that now: in particular, you mustn't distract yourself by thinking about it in ways whose only purpose is to prove it shouldn't have happened. I knew a very wise woman once. When anyone started in on the subject of what might have been, she always cut them off with, 'What might have been, wasn't; get on with your life.' Now, admittedly, I've known you only since you walked in that door, so feel free to tell me I'm wrong. But as I've listened to you, it seems to me — let me say it rather bluntly — that it's your preoccupation with proving negligence that's bogging down your progress through the stages of grief. You haven't accepted your husband's — Fred's — death; you're still mired in trying to assign blame for it. Is that too strong?"

"I think it is," she said. "It's certainly not abnormal for me to resent negligence on other people's part. And I don't think I'm consumed by the subject or obsessive about it. It's just that it shouldn't be allowed to slip by unchallenged — for the sake of other possible victims, if nothing else."

"What have you actually done about pursuing the matter?" I asked her.

"Well, I've seen two lawyers, but they don't seem to have found enough to go on. So I'll just keep trying. There's nothing wrong with trying, is there?"

"Maybe not. But then again, maybe yes. Since you can't bring Fred back, the only way you can answer that question is to measure the effect it's having on you. You think this whole business is doing you a favor?"

"If it helps other people, yes."

"But you came in here because you knew you weren't getting through your grief. You had a *problem*. All I'm suggesting is that the hunt for someone to blame might be part of that problem."

She thought about that for a while. "It's possible, of course," she said, "but I don't see it that way. What am I supposed to do? Repress my resentment and just let it fester? Or get it out into the open and do something about it?"

"Look," I answered. "Psychology is not my department — and you certainly didn't come here to listen to an amateur talk about it. For whatever reason, you came to me as a priest. So I owe you something of an apology for the tone of this conversation so far: too much home-brewed talk about possible psychological causes of your difficulty and not enough of what I'm really here for. Let me try to remedy that, all right?"

"All right. But I have to tell you, I'm not much more of a believer than my husband was. I'm certainly not a practicing Christian, though I do believe in God as a force for good."

"Okay. Let me talk about your problem in my own terms. Just do me the favor of remembering that from here on out I'm not saying a word about defects in your personality or your psychological makeup. All I'm talking about is what I saw from my own point of view. You came in here, right? And you were genuinely upset by the continuing grief you couldn't shake. Through the opening phases of our conversation, I saw that plainly.

113

But then, as you got onto the subject of negligence — and of trying to fix blame for it on somebody — I got a mental picture of something else: a picture of someone walking backward, for whatever reason, toward a cliff — of someone on a course that would do her no favors at all.

"Now what I'm about to say to you will make no sense unless you understand why I'm saying it. I'm not saying it because I want to talk about what you do or don't believe, or even about what you should or shouldn't believe. I may have some opinions about such things, but in the long run they're your business, not mine. And I'm not saying it because it's what I think you want to hear. As a matter of fact, I'm practically certain that what I'm going to say won't be anything you expected at all. The only reason I'm saying it is because I myself actually believe it. What you do with it after that is entirely up to you. Fair enough?"

She nodded.

"Good. A while back, I said you came to me as a priest. Now I don't know what that means to you, but what it means to me in this particular context is that you came to me as an authentic witness to the Gospel — the Good News of what God has done for the world in Jesus. And as I read the Gospel, it's the exact opposite of what most people — including a lot of preachers — think it is. They think it's some kind of religious recipe for getting their act together — for solving their problems or straightening up their lives so that God will approve of them and they can approve of themselves. Above all, they think it's about getting rid of the problems of evil and guilt — about doing something to avoid being judged, whether by God, or by others, or by themselves.

"But it isn't anything like that. That's all perfectly intelligible stuff the world has always been capable of telling itself — and of driving itself nuts with because none of it is really possible. It's all *bad* news, not Gospel. Religious recipes seldom get anybody's act together — and they never get it to a point where it can't be messed up in some new way. Problems that get solved are just replaced by new ones that may never be solved. Approval depends on the approver, not on anything the approvee does: if the approver's standards are high enough, approval never comes. And as far as evil is concerned, whatever it is that God has done in Jesus, he certainly hasn't done much about taking evil out of circulation.

"Furthermore, on the face of the Gospel it seems that God isn't the least bit interested in any of that intelligible but pointless stuff. Instead, he waltzes into the world and makes the weird announcement that he's simply dropped the whole business. He says he's come not to judge but to save. He says not that he's going to deal with guilt but that because of what he's done, there just isn't any guilt left. He says you can't deal with evil by resisting it, only by forgiving it. He says, in other words, that the whole of the world's habitual way of operating in those departments is upside down. And he says that in Jesus he's made a whole new right-side-up world — and that that's the only real world, the only one that can be a lasting, happy place.

"Our problem, of course, is that we're so used to standing on our heads that when he shows up, we think he's the one who's upside down. If the Gospel is proclaimed correctly, therefore, it's always going to sound nuts to us. As a matter of fact, it will always sound wrong, and immoral, and threatening to all the values we know and love even though they're killing us. Let me give you a couple of instances.

"In one of his parables, Jesus depicts the God character as a farmer who refuses to let his workers pull the evil weeds out of his wheat field. 'Let them be,' he says. (The Greek verb he uses is the word for *forgive;* what he's saying is that for all the time of the history of the world, God isn't going to do anything about getting evil out of the mix — and that we shouldn't, either.) And later on he tells a whole string of parables in which the characters who are held up for praise are all evildoers (like the prodigal son and the tax collector), and the so-called good characters (like the prodigal's elder brother and the Pharisee) are all given a hard time. Therefore

— since it's the sleazy heroes who show how Jesus thinks God really acts — he's talking about a God who doesn't fit anybody's idea of how a genuine God ought to behave. The God who's revealed in the Gospel is just too laid back on the subject of evil to qualify for membership in the God Union. He is not a scorekeeper. He does not insist on his pound of flesh. He does not go after sinners with a stick. Instead, he forgives. And on the cross — in the death of Jesus — his final word on the subject of all our sins and all our guilt is simply to shut up about it forever.

"Bear with me one minute more. I told you I saw you backing toward a cliff when you latched onto the business of finding somebody to blame for your husband's death. The cliff was unforgiveness. And just as it's one of the laws of the old universe that you can't walk over the edge of the Grand Canyon without paying a price, it's one of the laws of the New Creation in Jesus (as a matter of fact, it's practically the supreme law) that you can't hang onto blame and unforgiveness without paying a price. That's just going against the grain of the only universe that can last. And the price you're paying for working at cross' purposes with that new universe is the crippling of the new life you could be enjoying right now — the stalling of it in the old order of vengeance and blame. It's that, and not your grief, that's your problem. Your grief will run its course all by itself, provided you don't do anything to interrupt its course. But you've put a block under its wheels. And that block is your persistent fuss over who's to blame. If you get that out of the way, your life will roll slowly but surely into newness. If you don't — or for as long as you don't — you will never really accept Fred's death. And if you don't accept his death, your grief will go right on being the incomprehensible problem you brought in here in the first place. Does any of that make sense to you?"

She frowned. "Well! Your ideas of God are certainly different."

"They're not different. It's the world's ideas of God that are different. What I'm trying to tell you is that according to the Gospel, what you call 'my ideas' are simply authentic: they represent what God in Christ has actually revealed himself to be like — they're what Christianity really teaches, as opposed to what most people, including a lot of Christians in a lot of ages, have thought it teaches. God is simply not the infinite guilt-monger we've made him out to be. He's called off the whole guilt game for lack of interest on his part, and he's invited us to enjoy life without it. That's why the Gospel is Good News: because everything else people believe about God is bad news — a recipe for a miserable life, presided over by a misery-peddling bookkeeper. Do you see the point? You and I never got around to the subject of your own possible guilt over Fred's death because we got detoured by your obsession with blaming somebody else for it. But that guilt is probably there, isn't it? I mean, look! Not coming back from your conference when he landed in the hospital with a heart problem! That's a guaranteed guilt-producer. And while I'm being tough, I might as well say that you struck me as fencing yourself off from it with a lot of explanations and plausible reasons — and you latched onto the subject of negligence so you'd have yet another distraction from it. But my real point is that even if you, and the doctor, and the hospital are all as guilty as hell — even if you murdered him in his sleep with a carving knife — *God just isn't keeping score.* He's absolved Hitler; he's absolved all the child molesters and wife beaters in history; and he's absolved all of us before, during, and after our sins — in advance, free of charge, and forever. For the umpteenth time, therefore, he's dropped the subject, and he's invited you to drop it too and join the fun. I know that sounds crazy. But why don't you just decide to believe it and see what happens? How much fun is the sanity of your bookkeeping giving you?"

She frowned again. "I just don't know if I can do that. As I said, I'm not exactly a person who's been comfortable with the subject of faith."

"So forget about being comfortable. Look. If you were in a burning building and I told you to jump out the window into my

117

arms, what would be the point of telling me you're not comfortable with that? You're already terminally uncomfortable in the flames. You don't have to have some special predisposition in order to trust somebody. You don't even have to be free of doubts as to whether what he's telling you will work. All you have to do is decide to trust and then jump. The rest of the story (if it's true: I'll grant you that much) is somebody else's business, not yours. But if it is true, you're home free. What have you got to lose?"

She smiled. "That's a pretty hard sell for a subject like faith."

"You're a tough customer. We deserve each other."

"But I wouldn't even know where to begin."

"You begin by deciding to trust the wacky new order of forgiveness in Jesus. That much, only you can do. I can point you to it, and I can tell you that the sensible old order you currently trust is a loser. But I can't make the decision to trust for you. If you do make it, though, I think I can give you a couple of suggestions about how to proceed. You want me to try?"

"I guess so — if a conditional Yes is enough."

"Anything is enough as long as it's not nothing. Okay. First, every time you find yourself getting wound up on the subject of negligence in connection with Fred's death (other people's negligence, or even your own, if it comes up), I want you to say the Lord's Prayer. And I want you to pay particular attention to the words *'Forgive us our trespasses, as we forgive those who trespass against us.'* I want you to say those words as an act of forgiveness to everybody, yourself included. And then, as soon as you're done with the prayer, get up and get moving into something you have to put your mind to: in other words, change the subject.

"Second, don't talk about the negligence business with anybody but me. I'll make an exception for your lawyer, if he still thinks he can make a case for it. But if he ever tells you as a professional that there's no point in pursuing the matter, take his word for it and don't go hunting for some ambulance-chaser who'll take it on. Outside of that, though, drop the subject with your friends and relatives, and don't let them get you onto it. Just tell them it upsets you too much, that you've done all you can about it, and that you'd appreciate their not bringing it up. Be firm about that.

"Third, if you do get to the point where you feel you've got to talk about it, make an appointment to come here and talk to me. In the meantime, I'm going to give you an image I think will help. You came in here with your grief. That was real, and it still is — and it's perfectly legitimate because it's a part of you, part of your life. But you also came in here lugging a suitcase full of bricks called guilt and blame and unforgiveness — and that wasn't legitimate because it's not (or at least it shouldn't be) part of your life. It's nothing but an impediment to your life: you keep picking it up at all hours of the day and night and letting it ruin your style. So what I want you to do is *leave that suitcase here in this office when you go.* If you get a desperate urge to lug it around again, you know where it is. And if you do come, I'll let you lug it all you like — reserving my right, of course, to try to convince you that you're crazy. But otherwise, every time you get even close to the subjects in it, remind yourself you haven't got it with you and do something else. There! A three-point program. What do you think?"

"I almost thought for a minute there you were going to tell me you'd do something with the suitcase if I left it here."

"What I do with it is irrelevant for now. The only thing that matters is that you keep reminding yourself you don't have it. Whether I try in some mystical way to bear the burden of its contents for you, or just leave it in my closet and don't go near it with a ten-foot pole — that's something we can talk about another day. The one question you have to answer at this moment is, 'Will you leave it here?'"

"I suppose I could try."

"Not good enough. This is a game, for heaven's sake. And, like all games, it has to be taken seriously or it's no fun. Either you go by the rules, or you're not playing at all. How about it?"

She was silent for a good while. Then she said, "If I say Yes, may I at least tell my friend Marta what you've said to me, and what you've suggested I do?"

"Yes. But just once; and as soon as you can. Then get on with the program: forgiveness all around, no talking about the negligence, and no sneaking down here and taking the suitcase out for a walk."

I got up, went over to her chair, and took her hand.

"You drive a hard bargain," she said, smiling again.

"Hard, maybe. But a bargain, definitely. There's a whole new life out there, with all of the old one — good, bad, and indifferent — remembered in love and forgiveness. It really is Good News. When you're ready, give me a ring and we'll talk again."

The Second Session

She was late again. After a few pleasantries about the dreadfulness of the weather, I reopened the subject. "All right, Mabel. Why don't you begin by telling me where you are right now. How have you been managing with what we talked about last time?"

"Not too well, I'm afraid, Robert. I'm still breaking down in tears, and I still can't seem to put the circumstance of my husband's death to rest. I have a feeling I'm wearing my friends' patience thin. They don't bring the matter up anymore; and when I do, they try to get off it as quickly as they can."

"How have you made out with the program I suggested? Have you said the Lord's Prayer when you found yourself drifting into the subject?"

"I've done that sometimes. But most often, I find myself very far into the subject before I even realize what's happening."

"Well," I said, "that's to be expected. It's never easy. Do I take it, then, that the other two parts of the program — not talking about it, and not picking up the suitcase of bricks — haven't been roaring successes, either? I must say, though, you're a good burglar: if you broke in here and took the suitcase for a walk, you left no signs of forcible entry."

She brightened a little. "You're right. I really haven't stopped worrying the subject like a dog with a bone. It's interesting. When I went home after I last talked with you, I did as you said and told Marta, as best I could, what you'd said to me. And for the first time, I felt a little better about it all. But after that, I sort of slipped back into the old pattern."

"That's natural too, I think. As a matter of fact, it's the reason I suggested you talk to Marta about it only once. The first time around, I was pretty sure you'd be securely inside yourself, working hard at explaining more or less objectively what this crazy priest had said to you. Later on, though, when that effort wasn't uppermost in your mind, it'd be much easier for you to slip back into the distractions."

"I'm sorry," she said. "It's just harder than anyone seems to think."

"Of course it is. You're the one who actually has to break the pattern. The rest of us are just bystanders who may or may not be helpful. Speaking of helpful, though, something just occurred to me. Maybe one of the reasons you felt better explaining what I said to Marta had nothing to do with the objectivity it gave you. Maybe it was just the fact of having talked with a male about your problems. From what you've said, it seems you haven't been doing much of that. All the conversations you've referred to seem to have been with women friends."

"That's true. But that's mostly who my friends are."

"There's nothing wrong with that. But no matter how self-contained Fred was, and no matter how much you were apart, having a man to talk to was part of your life for nineteen years. Maybe it just felt comfortable to hear a male voice again. Maybe it still does: you're back here for another go-around. You know something? It might be a good idea, if you have any male friends you can talk to easily, to make use of them at this point. And not just for the comfort. You've had maleness in your life for a long time. It's possible, of course, that you'd like to chuck the whole lot of us. But it's also possible that one of the keys to reinstalling the past in your new life could be a welcoming back of male companionship. Not the widow-on-the-prowl bit — unless that appeals to you — but maybe a little time spent in the presence of voices an octave lower."

She grinned. "Thank you for the compliment, if it was one."

"Call it a suspicion that turned into a compliment. Anyway, moving right along: if it's all right with you, I'd like to go back and add to something I said last time — about guilt not being any part of the Gospel message."

She looked puzzled for a moment, then said, "Fine."

"Good. Because guilt — at least as we talk about it nowadays — is not in the New Testament. There's legal liability for actions taken, of course — like Jesus being guilty of blasphemy — and there's obviously the notion that bad actions have consequences for the actor. But the idea that we stand before God or anyone else as guilty, and therefore have to do something about our guilt before our relationships can get anywhere, simply isn't there. As far as God is concerned, he's dropped the subject and restored his relationship with us all by himself: in Jesus, he presumes us all innocent. And as far as our waiting for other people to get proven guilty or innocent is concerned, Jesus makes it perfectly clear that that's a no-no. Do you know the parable of the Unforgiving Servant? The one in which the servant's master forgives him a million-dollar debt, and then the servant goes out and beats up on a fellow servant who owes him ten bucks? Well, at the end of the story, when the master hears about it, he chews out the servant and has him delivered to the torturers — which is a bit rough from our point of view, but actually just a crisp, first-century way of saying the guy is totally wrong. What Jesus is saying, therefore, is that the only thing you can really do that's wrong is refuse to pass along the presumption of innocence you've already been blessed with. Or, to put it another way, the only thing you can really be guilty of is harping on guilt.

"Now if that's the New Testament case, where did all the centuries of Christian guilt-mongering come from? Well, the usual suspect who gets rounded up for starting it all is Augustine; but except for his preoccupation with sexual sins, he's not as guilty of peddling guilt as people think. It was actually medieval Christianity that invented the 300-horsepower guilt-spreader that's been running over us ever since. It was the medieval preoccupation with hell — and with the totally non-Gospel idea that good guys go to heaven and bad guys to hell — that convinced us that guilt was hazardous to our eternal health.

"That's all baloney, of course. There are no good guys in heaven, just forgiven sinners — guilty types whose guilt has been abolished free of charge. And there are no bad guys in hell, just more forgiven sinners — guilty types who stupidly refuse to accept the abolition of their guilt, and who for some reason find the thought of a free ride home an insult to their integrity.

"You might think, of course, that the Reformers — who rediscovered the New Testament notion of free, undeserved grace and forgiveness in the basement of the medieval church — would have scotched all that. But by and large they didn't. And that's because the only people available to run the Reformation were, every last one of them, late medievalists: even though they spotted the medieval church's outrages against grace, they never quite got a bead on the outrages it committed in the name of moralism. They never quite shook the idea that it was against God's principles to have any truck with evil. Even the Calvinists, who said that the goodness of God's elect had nothing to do with his choosing of them, ended up saying that the badness of the non-chosen was justly rewarded by his non-choosing of them. But saying that God would predestine some people to hell — after Jesus went out of his way to say he came to save them all — isn't Gospel. It's just moralism in theological drag.

123

"But anyway — and you've been very patient with this excursion into the history of theology — the net result has been that medieval guilt has come straight on through to modern times. It's remained a preoccupation for everybody, Christians included, even though nobody is guilty any more as far as the New Testament is concerned. As Paul says, 'There is therefore now no condemnation . . .' The blame business is over. The guilt shop is closed. And this theological bus ride is now at an end."

Mabel straightened in her chair and shook her head. "That's all very well for people who believe it. But not many do, apparently. Psychiatrists' offices are full of people who desperately need to deal with guilt. No matter what you say, it's a huge reality."

"I'm not denying that. I'm just trying to fill you in on how it got so huge. It got that way not because it had to but *because of a belief system that said it had to.* People talk as if Christianity is an unrealistic belief system because it thumps the tub for forgiveness and not resisting evil; and then they go on to praise the world's preoccupation with guilt and punishment as realism — as if it were not only the way things are but the way they ought to be. But don't you see? The world isn't preoccupied with reality at all: it's hung up on a belief system that runs contrary to all human experience. What's really made a mess of the world? Grace? Forgiveness? Turning the other cheek? Or is it guilt, punishment, vengeance, and retribution?

"Look. I sat here trying to sell you the idea of forgiving your husband's death and getting on with your life — of trusting, of believing that that's the way things really ought to be. And you kept saying you were uncomfortable with the idea of believing. But you're not uncomfortable with it: you're up to your eyebrows in it, and you're thinking it's the best thing since domestic hot water. The only trouble is that what you believe in is actually a stone-cold, God-awful system that will never give you a minute's comfort until you stop believing in it and trust something more pleasant."

"But psychiatry doesn't try to change people's beliefs. It just tries to get them to face the guilt or the blame they've repressed."

"I buy only part of that. Bringing repressed guilt or blame to the surface so it can be faced is a legitimate exercise. But it can have only two outcomes: either the guilt-slash-blame will turn out to be a misunderstanding (in which case, understanding will make it vanish — *tout comprendre, tout pardonner*); or it will turn out to be right on target (in which case, you still have to decide whether what you now understand should be punished or pardoned). And that decision depends entirely on the system you decide to believe in, not on the mere fact of getting what was repressed out in the open. If anything, therefore, psychiatry clears the ground for a re-examination of your beliefs. And unless you opt for believing in pardon, you might as well never have gotten down on the couch."

"Well, I never thought of it that way."

"I could be wrong, of course. You seem to have a knack for getting me off my subject onto yours — or else I'm more given to cocktail-party psychologizing than I like to think. But in any case, enough of that. Let me try to get us on a more positive track."

She smiled again. "You do remind me of Fred, you know. He had the same way of coming at me hammer and tongs about something and then backing off and changing the subject. I used to call him the Artful Dodger."

"Ah! Now it's my turn to accept a compliment. Thank you, Mabel. But seriously, you just got me onto the subject I was heading for: your relationship with your husband. First, though, let me give you another image.

"Years ago I used to shop regularly at a little neighborhood Greek delicatessen, the proprietor of which was something of a wag. One day I was behind a customer who was inspecting a trayful of *baklava* on the counter. It was summer, and there were quite a few flies on the pastry, so the woman said, 'The *baklava* looks good, but I don't like all those flies on it!' He said, 'So, fine. I won't charge you for the flies.' I've used that as an illustration ever since. Life is always calling us to make a decision between paying attention to the *baklava* and paying attention to the flies. And for some reason — probably going all the way back to Adam and Eve — most of us decide on the flies. As I see my job, therefore, it's waving away the flies so people can concentrate on what will really please them instead of standing there and getting pissed off at irrelevancies.

"I've tried to do that with your hunt for someone to blame for Fred's death — and with your own guilt, if any, over not coming home. All I want to add here is one more wave at one more fly. It seems to me that your not coming home was at least as much his doing as yours. Maybe it was even more his than yours. Maybe part of what you're struggling with is a resentment at being shut out of his death as a result of his being so insistent that you didn't have to come home because everything was hunky-dory.

"Let me take back the word 'resentment' and substitute 'frustrated longing.' Maybe, under all the mutual independence and not living on top of each other, you were always hoping for a kind of closeness that he, for his own reasons, wasn't able to allow. You've said, of course, that the 'distance' between you was basically to your liking. For part of your makeup, that was probably true. But for another, deeper part, maybe it wasn't. And so when you were deprived of that closeness at such an important time (by whoever's fault, it doesn't matter), it just hurt. Consequently, it went down into an undifferentiated bag of hurts that you labeled 'grief,' but that actually contained lots of other items as well."

"That's true," she said. "Fred was so . . . private. And I do think he was a bit driven about avoiding the subject of death. It was almost as if he thought that if he kept it out of his mind, he'd be able to keep it at bay indefinitely. Thank you. That helps."

"Good. Maybe it's worth pursuing. But not with me. Do you have a therapist you're seeing now?"

"Not at the moment."

"Well, think about it. That might help too. But back to my

department — yet again. The point I want to make is that the most important thing you have to do now — or whenever you get all this history sorted out to your liking — is to reinstall Fred, and your life with him, in your life now. You have to end the 'arm's length' fencing with it that's holding up your progress into a new life."

"But suppose I come up with the resentments or the frustrated longings you talked about. Suppose the relationship Fred and I had turns out not to have been the satisfactory thing I've always told myself it was. How do you reinstall something like that? Why would you even bother?"

"You'd bother because, whatever it was, it's part of you. You can't cut it off without cutting off part of yourself, of your own history. Besides, it's not going to turn out to have been all bad — not unless you fake it. You're an intelligent person: you couldn't possibly have misread everything.

"So that leaves your first question: 'How do I reinstall the bad stuff and not have it mess up my life all over again?' And for that, I have another illustration. Tell me something first, though. How much experience of the Episcopal Church do you have?"

"Not much, I'm afraid."

"Have you ever been to a Eucharist — a Communion service?"

"Yes."

"Good enough. Now, did it ever strike you that the whole business of remembering Jesus' death and receiving his body and blood is a very peculiar way of spending a weekend morning?"

"It certainly did. It sounds for all the world like cannibalism."

"That's not what I had in mind. Consider the scene in church on a Sunday. Here are a bunch of people, more or less dressed to the nines, in an expensive building, with maybe very spectacular music and even a paid choir, *deliberately celebrating the worst thing the human race — which includes them — has ever done: the murder of God Incarnate.*

127

"Do you see the point? They've taken the rottenest thing that ever happened and reinstalled it in their lives as a joyful remembrance. They haven't run away from the evil; they've actually made it the centerpiece of their celebration. They've taken what should have caused only alienation, and, by the pardon that flows from it to them, they've turned it into a festival of reconciliation."

"But I don't know if I believe that. The reconciliation, I mean."

"You could decide to. We're back at faith again, you see. In the long run, it's the only product I've got in the store."

"The hard sell again."

"Naturally. Let me give you one last illustration. Did you ever see a Nerf ball? One of those little, spongy jobbies that comes with a kid's basketball hoop you can hang on the top of a door?"

"Yes. I think so."

"Well, sometimes, when I want to drive home what I believe the Gospel really says about the reconciliation, I take a Nerf ball into the pulpit and tell the congregation I want them to think of it as my life — my whole existence, from birth to whenever. Then I tell them there are two grips on that ball — on my life. The first is mine. So I take the ball in my right hand and poke all kinds of dents in it, and I scrunch it up in my hand so it's not even a nice, round ball anymore, just a mess — just the way my life, as I hold it, so often is. But then I tell them that the other grip on the ball is Jesus' grip — and that in his grip, my life is no longer a mess in any way. And to demonstrate that, I place my left hand over my right, and I slowly let go of my compressing grip on the ball and slip my right hand out from under my left. Presto! The ball is now in my left hand — the 'Jesus' hand — and it's a nice, round, reconciled ball again.

"Then I come to the punch line: those two grips on the ball — right-handed and left-handed, mine and Jesus' — *are going on at the same time.* All I have to do is get my grip out of the way, and his grip will have me reconciled.

128

"And so for the clincher, I ask the congregation what that says about the life of faith. I usually get blank looks, so I go right ahead. Once again I scrunch up the ball in my right hand; but then I take a piece of plastic wrap, put it over my right hand, and put my left hand back over the whole shooting match. Then I say, 'The plastic wrap is unbelief, and the life of faith consists of two things only. First, you get rid of the barrier of unbelief' (I pick up a corner of the plastic wrap with my teeth and pull it out); 'and second, you let go of your grip on your life' (I go back to the first part of the demonstration and remove my right hand so my left holds a round ball again).

"So, for what it's worth, there's my positive contribution to what's bothering you. Your life, my life, Fred's and your life together, mine and my children's, mine and my impossible brother-in-law's — all of them are held in two grips: our own, which is a loser; and Jesus', which is a winner. If you get the unbelief out and let go of your own, damaging grip, it's all okay right now. You're reconciled in Jesus. There's nothing you need to do, just a couple of things you need to stop doing. So stop already. And enjoy."

"You make it sound like Zen."

"Zen do it. And with my profoundest apologies for ending on a pun, I really do have to run now. Give me a ring whenever you want to talk again."

Mabel Perkins moved away shortly afterward. Months later she mailed back a book I'd lent her with a note of thanks but no word as to how she was doing. I've never seen or heard from her since.

EIGHT

The Mystery and Grief

OTTO: For a hard sell, that wasn't much of a sale. From start to finish, I'd say you got her to move about an eighth of an inch.

LOUISE: I think Robert did very well, considering. She's not what I would call a warm person. She had some feelings, of course; but she seemed almost totally consumed by what she had in her head. And she called her husband driven! Maybe the poor man died of having to live with her dog-with-a-bone disposition.

ALICE: She certainly was self-centered. I tried to keep count of how often she actually referred to her husband by name. Twice is all I can remember. She did say he was brilliant, of course. But even that seemed as if she was talking about a possession: brilliant like a diamond I keep in my bureau drawer. For the rest, it was all *her* work, *her* friends, *her* conferences, *her* crusade about the negligence. Stubborn!

ENID: Or locked up, at least. Given her profession, I kept waiting for a little psychological insight to break through somewhere. Of course, psychologists are often just as dense as their patients; but if she ever did have a clue, she kept it well hidden. It's as if there was a wall around her — a wall she didn't even suspect was there. You realize, Robert, that right at the start you asked her to call you by your first name? But except for once in the second session, I don't think she ever called you anything. The lady has *insulation!* And her first reaction to everything is to make sure her insulation is in place, not to respond to the person she's talking with.

ROBERT: Mabel doesn't seem to be getting rave reviews, does she?

FRANK: I don't know. She wasn't all that bad. What I liked best, though, was the way you dealt with her. You didn't let her personality influence your attitude toward her. Sure, you came on a little strong about the things you thought were interfering with her progress. But aside from that, you didn't sit in judgment of her. And you certainly did try to sell her on faith, so you get high marks in my book for not letting her get you off the track. After all, she's just one more sinner who needs to believe in Jesus. Her personality may be getting in her way; but then, whose isn't?

ROBERT: Thank you, Frank. It's fascinating. You and I managed to end up together last time, and today we've even started out in the same place! You've summed up my convictions about pastoral counseling perfectly. When I deal with individual human beings, I think my job as a priest is to keep my eye on two things. The first is the ball of faith; the second is the people themselves as they stand in the batter's box and swing at the ball. I'm a *coach* — not a psychologist, or a magician, or even a healer. Those are jobs for other professionals. Of course, if I can manage to get in a few amateurish licks at such crafts, well and good. But they're not my profession: my job is inviting people to believe the Good News.

So it's none of my business if they come in insulated, or if they're boring, or arrogant, or locked up — or even if they leave my office in the same shape they came. I'm there to apply the Gospel to their condition "whether they will hear, or whether they will forbear." Everything else is their business.

OTTO: That's all true enough. But isn't it possible you moved a bit too fast from her grief to the Gospel? Mabel is still no prize in my book; but then, you weren't exactly the warm, comforting parson she expected.

ROBERT: Granted. But I am what I am, and I call 'em as I see 'em. I can't give her somebody else's version of help.

ENID: I understand that. But do you know what surprises me, Robert? It's how little specific mention you make of the Mystery of Christ in your counseling sessions. With us, it's practically all you talk about. But with your counselees, you almost seem to be walking around it on tiptoe. Yet if anything is your version of help, that's certainly it. Don't you think you could be a little more direct about it?

ROBERT: Yes and no, Enid. Actually, it underlies everything I say, and I never feel I'm very far from it. But after all, it's a *doctrine* — an understanding of the Gospel — not the Gospel itself. Furthermore, it's a doctrine that's so far removed from what people usually understand the Gospel to be, I figure it's better to give them just the raw Gospel materials, not a bunch of interpretations that will only seem weird to them. That's why I mostly present them with the actions and parables of Jesus — which are quite weird enough. Citing Jesus at least makes it harder for them to write the Gospel off as "just doctrine." But only harder; not impossible, by a long shot.

132

ENID: It must be difficult. You never gave Mabel a chance to say whether she did or didn't know anything about the parables you referred to, but I have a suspicion she was . . . well, biblically at least, pretty much illiterate.

ROBERT: Probably. There are always so many things you can't assume people have — like knowledge of what Jesus actually said, or even the gist of his parables, let alone their real thrust. Mostly, they just have some vague idea that Jesus was an inspirational figure, like Kahlil Gibran. (Seriously. You have no idea how many times couples want to have Gibran read at weddings; when I tell them the lessons have to be from Scripture, they look at me as if I'm out of my mind. For them, Gibran and the Bible are the same thing.) But, in any case, the result is that the crucial idea behind the whole business of the Mystery of Christ — namely, that Jesus is really God Almighty in human flesh — isn't even entertainable by them. As far as they're concerned, it's just bizarre — something no educated person believes anymore. Consequently, either I just state it as my own crazy belief, or I omit it entirely and play whatever catch-up ball I can manage.

OTTO: Yes. With bits of off-the-cuff psychology, and illustrations thrown around like confetti, and even the occasional Greek storekeeper tossed in for good measure. Actually, though, it's not a bad mixture: at least it keeps them off balance.

ROBERT: Well, one of the things I am is an old classroom teacher; and once you've been in that trade, you never quite shake the habit of trying to improve the mind of whoever's in front of you. My wife says I can't even stand to watch someone dicing celery without suggesting a better way of doing it. So one of the things I'm always up to in counseling is trying to correct people's misapprehensions of Christianity. That's why I keep tossing them Jesus, and his parables, and the central acts of his life — like his death and resurrection: they simply haven't heard anything *authentic* about such things. Even if they were exposed to them in Sunday School (which is a big assumption), what they probably got was a lot of lukewarm pap about sweet Jesus and the boy Samuel at prayer. For my money, what we call "Christian education" is almost always mismanaged. Either it's sentimental piety, or it's a lot of doctrinal answers to questions the kids have never raised. In any case, it's so heavily edited (the rough parts of the Old Testament left out, Jesus turned into Mr. Nice, his parables watered down to lessons in loveliness) that authentic Christianity just never gets through to them.

My idea of Christian education, therefore, is to give them the straight, unedited stuff: just the stories, exactly as they were told — with the urge to explain them, or to explain them away, firmly strapped in the back seat. Children's minds are an empty gallery, with no biblical pictures on the walls at all. Our job is simply to hang up the pictures in that gallery. Then, later on in life, when they happen to wander through the gallery, at least the original, weird masterpieces will be there for them to look at again — and maybe they'll see things they've never noticed before. But if all you give them is the Infant Jesus in velvet pants, or a lot of stuff labeled "religion," they'll just figure it's too tame to have anything to do with the wildness and weirdness of life as they actually experience it.

LOUISE: But what about comfort? That's not completely out of the question, is it?

ROBERT: No. But you have to be careful what you hand out in the name of comfort. The temptation is to say something people expect — something that amounts to "if you trust God enough, he'll make it all go away and give you a nice, comfortable life again." But that's not the Gospel. Jesus saves the world not by being a masterpiece of comfort but by his own terminal *discomfort* on the cross. And he tells us to take up our cross — our own discomfort — and follow him along the same road. He never once announced that it would be his program to make discomfort disappear from the face of the earth — at least not any time before the last day.

Instead, he gives us his assurance that he's *with us in our discomfort.* "Comfort" comes from the Latin root *fort-,* which means "strength." What he really gives us, therefore, is the strength that comes from trusting that no matter what happens to us — sins, guilt, diseases, death — nothing can separate us from *him.* Thus, *he* is the strength — not some baseless hope that it will all go away like a bad dream.

ENID: I think we're drifting. I'd like you to get back to Mabel. I don't quite see how you could be so sure that her pursuing the possibility of negligence in connection with her husband's death was at the heart of her not being able to get through the grief process.

OTTO: Yes. If it rang any bells with her, she certainly didn't let on while she was talking with you — and not ever, if her subsequent behavior is any indication.

ROBERT: Well, I wasn't *sure.* But I had a suspicion it was at least possible that the distraction of a lawsuit could be stalling her progress. For her to concentrate on proving that Fred's death shouldn't have happened could easily have been a way of keeping death at arm's length — of not letting the fact of it be installed in her life. Or, to put it correctly, of not recognizing the fact that it was already installed and she was fighting it.

First of all, death is the great sacrament of the Mystery of Christ: it's the engine of the New Creation. (It also happens to be the engine of the old creation as well. Everything that's alive lives by the death of other living beings — even vegetarians live by killing off carrots; and for just one other instance, if it weren't for the death of thousands of years' worth of leaves, there wouldn't be any topsoil out there, just sand.) In addition, death is the centerpiece of the church's two great sacraments: in Baptism, we say that the candidate is "buried with Christ in his death"; and in the Eucharist, there's so much death-talk that Mabel's chief reaction to it was that it sounded like cannibalism. So Christians, far from running away from death, or trying to prove it's a pussycat instead of a man-eating tiger, have actually installed it as the hallmark of their liturgy.

You're all old enough to remember what funerals were like before the liturgical movement: black vestments; lots of gloomy hymns; sermons about how the "loved one" had just gone on to another place (as if death were no different from moving to Scranton); too much talk about the immortality of the soul (as if the minute your insignificant old body conked out, your soul would float straight up to God without any help from Jesus); and, in general, very little real comfort for anybody with the wit to recognize that the corpse they were burying was a person they were going to miss like mad. Do you see? Back in those "good old days," the church had pretty much lost its Christian nerve on the subject of death. And even the new Prayer Book, while it's cut down on the use of the word "body," can't quite steel itself to use the word "corpse." But a dead body simply isn't a body anymore: it's just stuff that was once a body lying where it fell. It's a corpse; and, as such, its parts will sooner or later all go their own ways.

But I'm distracting myself. My point was that funerals

136

now are supposed to be more Christian than all that. The theme is death and resurrection, not airy-fairy philosophy or avoiding the issue. And we wear white and sing Easter hymns because dear old Fred is really dead and really risen — as he has been all along in Jesus. That's why we urge people to have a celebration of the Eucharist at funerals: so that our installation of Fred's death in our lives can get a helping hand from our habitual, sacramental installation of the death of Jesus that's at work in us. It's all much more realistic now. It's based on what we really and distinctively believe — on our authentic faith, not on our incidental philosophy.

ENID: I still think we're drifting. I think Mabel's own guilt is the root of her problem. The negligence suit is more a distraction from *that* than it is from death. Just think about it. She had not one but two opportunities to come home: when she decided to stay at the conference, and when she decided to visit a friend after it was over. I mean, really! Even if her husband wasn't critical, hospitals are still boring, difficult places to put up with. In fact, it's only if you're so sick you're out of it that you *don't* want visitors. If you're out of the ICU and in a private room, you'd love to have your wife's company, with all its opportunities for comfortable small talk about normal life. I think they had a very peculiar relationship. Maybe they didn't even like each other very much. So maybe, deep down, her not coming to him was just one more episode in their continuing standoff — another one of her punitive reactions to his inaccessibility, to his shutting her out.

ROBERT: Ah! That's a psychological analysis I didn't think of. But it still boils down to the same thing. Even after you've pinpointed your guilt to a fare-thee-well, you still have to decide what you're going to do about it: lug it around, or accept the fact that since God has forgiven you, you might as well forgive

137

yourself. The one thing you mustn't decide to do is go on trying to prove you're a nice guy and therefore not guilty. All that does is leave you a sitting duck for getting into the same mess all over again.

You know why marriage is a sacrament? What it's a sacrament *of?* It's not a sign of some peculiar state called matrimony that applies only to male/female couples who've made scout's-honor promises. It's a sacrament of *all relationships,* beginning with the relationship of Christ to the New Creation that is his Bride and going all the way down through the relationships of lovers (straight or gay), of parents and children, of single people and their friends — and, for all I know, of ducks and drakes.

Maybe the church singled out marriage because it's the most difficult of all relationships. As anyone who's ever been married knows full well, marriage is practically impossible. It shoves us out shivering into the cold light of the fact that it's not *what we do* that so regularly pisses people off, it's *who we are.* We spend our lives, of course, pretending it's the other way around: that anyone who's halfway decent should be as comfortable with the cut of our jib as we are — should see us as the perfect peaches we believe ourselves to be. But then reality hits us: our whining about how we have every right to expect dinner on time, or to want the thermostat left up at night (or our pouty, self-pitiful giving up on such desires), isn't met with cheers and beers. It's met with the charge that we're nothing but rotten eggs — selfish, bossy manipulators whom nobody could possibly live with. And that will always come as a shock to us until we understand that it's *us* they can't stand, not just our behavior.

What it all adds up to is that any real reconciliation is way beyond us — even if we can manage to get all glued together psychologically. No marriage — no human relationship of any kind — can survive in the old order of guilt and blame. (I take back my remark about ducks: they seem not to need a reconciliation.) Relationships can survive only in the New Order of the Mystery of Christ — in the order of grace and forgiveness. Or, better said, people can survive relationships only in that order.

Forgiveness, therefore, is not a psychological matter, or a religious matter, or a "spiritual" matter: it's a *political* matter — it's the centerpiece of the politics of the New Order. Politics is the art of the possible. And the only thing we can possibly do with the impossible natures we foist on each other is drop dead to the business of proving we're perfect peaches and hand out pardon all around.

In a way, I'm sorry I didn't spend more time talking with Mabel about my suggestion that psychological analysis is only *preparation* for living, not living itself. Therapy has the same relationship to life that weight-lifting and body-building have to playing baseball: it may get you in good enough shape not to be defeated by the normal stresses of the game, but standing in the batter's box and actually being able to connect with an inside fastball is not something you learn on the couch or the Nautilus machine. Mabel's trouble was that she wasn't a politician. She was an ideologue: ideas and rules and analysis were her cup of tea; if she could talk herself into thinking something was right, that was the end of it for her. But being right — even being really right — is no guarantee you can make your relationships work. Only political wisdom can enable you to do that. And in the New Order, to say it once more, the only politically wise thing to do is forgive — which, unfortunately, is the one thing the ideologue's ideology can't accept. The world is dying of rightness; it can live only if it drops dead to the subject and lets grace abound.

ALICE: So trusting the New Order really is everything. We're back to faith again. All Mabel really had to do was believe.

FRANK: That's right. You know, Robert, little by little you're actually getting through to me. People might think that a person like me, raised in the evangelical tradition, is even less likely to change than Mabel was. But I'm beginning to see that my constant fretting about works has been distracting me from the freedom that comes when we take seriously salvation by faith alone. All that fuss over rightness — and especially all that panic over the danger of doing something wrong — amounts to nothing more than a recipe for saving yourself instead of letting Jesus do it.

ROBERT: Don't feel you have to knock evangelicalism, Frank. There's plenty wrong with everybody's ecclesiastical tradition. But at least we all have the Bible and the apostolic witness, so there's also plenty right about us. As far as I'm concerned, nobody has to "convert" from one ecclesiastical tradition to another. We don't have to "move on," we just have to *listen*. "Evangelical" is simply an englishing of the Greek word for "Gospel," which means "good news." And as I said, the Gospel is always weird enough to break right through anything our particular traditions may have gotten wrong. The truth that makes us free is always ticking away like a time bomb in the basement of everybody's church. And that truth isn't a bunch of ideas. It's Jesus. Sooner or later, if we just sit still and listen, he'll blow the lid off any prison we've built.

ENID: One other thing. When you were talking to Mabel about the suitcase full of bricks, and how you'd keep it in your office for her, I couldn't help but think of Charles Williams' *Descent into Hell*. You know: Pauline, who's terrified because she keeps meeting herself coming down the street, comes to Peter Stanhope. I don't remember quite how the sequence of the book goes, but eventually she conquers her fear of the *Doppelgänger* by bearing the fear of an ancestor of hers who was burned at the stake four hundred years earlier. You made a passing allusion to possibly bearing the burden of the suitcase's contents for her. Did you have Williams in mind?

ROBERT: Yes. But I guess I figured it would have been one digression too many — or else that she would have gotten preoccupied with the idea as a gimmick and distracted herself once more from the business of faith. Or something like that.

ENID: But you're with *us* now. Do you actually think that sort of thing is possible? Or was it just more of Charles Williams' eccentricity?

ROBERT: Oh, no. Actually, I think it's quite centric. Even theologically sound, if you take the Mystery of Christ seriously. By the fact of the Incarnation, not only is God the Son in the world; the world is in God the Son. And if it's in him, it's right in the heart of the exchanges between the Persons of the Trinity. We make a reference to that every Sunday in the creed: we say we believe in the "communion of saints." The phrase goes all the way back to the Apostles' Creed, and the Fathers of the church made quite a big thing of it. All the members of the body of which Christ is the head are in relationship not only with him as head but with each other as members — just as the Persons of the Trinity always mutually indwell each other in act and essence. The doctrine the Fathers worked up went by the name of *perichoresis,* or *symperichoresis;* but in English it's usually expressed as "coinherence" — which, if you recall, is one of Charles Williams' pet ideas.

Anyway, the general idea as it applies to the bearing of burdens is that we're always in communion with each other. Even if one of us has been dead four hundred years, we're all still in the same room, so to speak. So when we pray for each other, for example, we don't have to get fussy about time or space. In Christ, we're all together. And in Christ, the saving grace of his whole work is always operative in every one of us. That's why we don't necessarily have to know what to pray for when we intercede.

Look. Suppose you died last Saturday night, but I didn't hear about it till Monday morning, so I prayed for your recovery at the Eucharist on Sunday. What am I supposed to do? Feel bad I got it wrong? Send God a cancellation prayer? Of course not. Maybe my prayer — in the coinherence, in the communion of saints — was the very thing that helped you face the terror of your death.

ENID: Retroactively?

ROBERT: Only from my point of view. From Christ's point of view, he's got the whole sequence all at once in the heart of the Trinity. He can rewire it frontward or backward as he likes. And the point is, he *likes*. He *cares*. All he wants us to do is let the energy of his liking and caring flow between us. He takes care of all the rest.

ENID: That's the most sensible explanation I've ever heard of why we pray for people. It doesn't get you all hung up on whether the particular prayer you prayed got a Yes, a No, or a Maybe from God. I might even start taking intercession seriously again.

ROBERT: Good! Another convert just by sitting still.

FRANK: There is one more thing I wonder about. When you were suggesting that Mabel leave the suitcase in your office, she said she'd try, and you said that wasn't good enough — that

142

this was all a game. You did say it had to be taken seriously, of course. But I guess the idea of faith as a *game* was too jarring for me. And it all went by so fast that it was just confusing.

ROBERT: All I had in mind at the time I said that, Frank, was my three-point program for her. But, having thought about it since then, I've decided that faith really *is* a game. It's a gamble, a leap, a vault into another order of reality — and all of those are elements in any game. Games are the most serious things in the world. Think with me about that for a bit. To play a game, the first thing you have to do is suspend the rules of the world you're living in and accept the rules of the new world of the game. For instance. If you came to the Monopoly board determined to live by the rules of ordinary life, there would be no reason why, if you wanted to land on Park Place, you couldn't just elbow everybody out of the way and put yourself there. But in the game you can't do that because you've set those rules aside in favor of new ones — and you allow yourself to be bound by them.

That's why it didn't matter whether I was talking about faith or about some two-bit pastoral counseling game. They're both the same kind of thing: a new order you have to submit to — to *trust* and act in accordance with. My hope was that if she went along with my suggestion about the suitcase, it would be a kind of preparation for going along with Jesus' suggestions about forgiveness. Come to think of it, maybe that was the real reason I shuffled off her question about what I'd do with the suitcase: I didn't want her to get distracted by the thought that I was working on an advanced degree in coinherence. But anyway, that's probably enough of that. Why don't we call it quits for today?

OTTO: No Doxology?

ROBERT: Not this time. Instead, why don't we offer a nice, non-specific, coinherent prayer for Mabel? Join me.

"Our Father, who art in heaven . . ."

NINE

Stephanie

Time now for a pastoral conversation with a different provenance. What follows in this chapter occurred neither in my office nor at the church door: I met Stephanie at the far end of a grand piano at a cocktail party. She was in her late twenties, darkish blonde, and well inside the boundaries of attractive. We were introduced by Thelma, one of those officious ladies who, if they are not already real-estate brokers, are probably destined to become such: their mission in life is matching up people they think have something to buy or sell. The commodity for sale, though, is apparently a matter of indifference to them — as is the sale itself, since more often than not they mindlessly lump together two sellers. Facilitation is the only thing they're interested in; and Thelma, having facilitated she knew not what, flitted away from Stephanie and me with the assurance that since we were both interested in "spiritual things," we would no doubt have a great deal to say to each other.

❦   ❦

So there we were at the piano, glasses of white wine in hand, left to make conversation over a trayful of bacon-wrapped dates. I slid the platter toward her and asked if she'd like one.

"Absolutely not," she said. "I'm a vegetarian."

"Well!" I said. "That's a coincidence. I'm an Episcopalian, and I'm not eating them, either. To tell the truth, though, I'm actually a member of the Anti-Finger-Food Church: my brand of Protestantism insists on a place at the table and food on a plate. Dining is almost dead among us, and cocktail-party nibbling is about to finish it off completely. This whole performance is only half a notch above eating Pop-tarts out of the toaster."

"Then what you really are is a Food Snob. I understand you've written a cookbook."

"Four, if you want the full number of my sins; plus the introduction to a book on Japanese Temple cuisine. Strictly vegetarian, that was: absolutely brilliant cooking, and totally incredible presentation. My wife and I went to Tokyo to get background on it. The abbess of the convent gave me an A in cooking but only a B- in arrangement. Besides being a bit color-blind, I also failed to inherit my father's artistic eye."

"Then your other cookbooks aren't vegetarian?"

"No. I'm sorry to say that's one church that won't have me; I cook and eat just about everything — though I am a great admirer of Armenian Lenten cuisine, which is totally vegetarian except for a bit of fish. My only standard for food is that it should taste good. When it comes to vegetables, I prefer them cooked by cooks, not religionists."

"You *are* dogmatic, aren't you."

"Only about food. Try me on something else."

"Okay. Reincarnation. What do you think about that?"

"It's at least a possibility. I'm certainly not about to tell you God couldn't have arranged the world that way if he, she, or it wanted to. And there's no doubt that there are plenty of people who think he did."

"But the church is against reincarnation, right?"

"Not the Episcopal Church, thank God. We've been too busy with sex to have any energy left over for other things. Personally,

146

though, I don't even like official pronouncements about sex: I draw the line on what people are supposed to subscribe to after the 'Amen' at the end of the Creed. Beyond that point, I consider even Christian thinking to be an open ball game. So now it's your turn. What do *you* think about reincarnation?"

"I believe in it. But you can't get off the hook that easily. You know perfectly well that a lot of Christians think it's a terrible idea."

"True. I suppose they arrive at that conclusion because they think reincarnation somehow violates the principle of the uniqueness of each individual person. They wonder which of your several incarnations will be the one God finally resurrects you in."

"But if there isn't any death," Stephanie said, "then that doesn't apply: the person — the soul — continues through all the incarnations. And anyway, people who believe there is a resurrection still have the same problem: even if you think you have only a single life, the matter of the body you have changes completely every seven years. So which body gets raised? The one you had as a one-year-old? Or as an eight-year-old? Or as a teenager? Or the one you died in?"

"That's very good. You've hit on the commonest Christian misperception of both reincarnation and the resurrection. What a lot of Christians don't understand is that among those who subscribe to reincarnation, particularly among the Orientals, the 'soul' is a quasi-substance — a kind of compressed computer file, if you like, of the whole history of the person. So if God wanted, he could take that compressed file and unzip it at the resurrection, raising all the lives at once — past lives included."

"Well! You're not so dogmatic after all. So you believe in reincarnation?"

"I can't answer that without making a distinction. I may *think* that reincarnation is a possibility; but I *believe* only in Jesus. For me, faith has to be *trust in a person,* not the acceptance of a philosophy or a view of the universe. So, since I see reincarnation as a system, and not as something a person promised me, my acceptance of it would depend on two things. First, I would have to be satisfied that it could be proved as a fact; but, second and more important, I would then have to decide whether I thought it was a nice fact or a not-so-nice fact — whether it was consistent with what I thought a really attractive fact ought to look like. You, of course, have answered both those questions about reincarnation in the affirmative; I haven't. But neither you nor I can properly say we believe it or disbelieve it. It's just not a matter of *faith*."

"But isn't resurrection just as much a system, a philosophy, as reincarnation? As a matter of fact, it's always seemed to me that it's a system based on a fairy tale and therefore not very attractive to people who prefer something more factual."

"I don't think that's quite the case. Sure, resurrection has been viewed as a system, even by Christians. But in the long run the church has never sold it as such. Christians, despite what they believe, don't know beans about resurrection as a system. All they can really claim is that they trust Jesus, and that he happens to have promised to raise the dead — whatever that may mean. They hardly *know* anything. Even the question of whether Jesus himself actually rose from the dead is historically unverifiable: we have no evidence except from people who already trusted him, and we have no way of getting back there to dig up new evidence one way or another. So if you want to call it a fairy tale, you're free to do so. But, by the same token, others are just as free to call reincarnation a fairy tale."

"But what about people who've actually been regressed into past lives? There are lots of us."

"You've been regressed?"

"Once."

"What past life turned up?"

"I was the widow of a Gypsy king, and I died in a pogrom against Gypsies."

148

"Fair enough. But suppose I accept that. What does it *mean?* What's the significance of it to you?"

"Why does it have to have significance for me? If it was true, it was true — even if I never figure out what it means."

"Fair enough again. But obviously it's at least attractive to you, or you wouldn't be defending it. What's the attractiveness?"

"The working out of my karma. The idea that somehow I'm moving forward into a life that gets fuller and fuller."

"What about bad karma? On second thought, don't even bother answering that. Your ending up in another life as a duck would be just another part of the same general progress."

"Reincarnationists believe only that you might have started out as a lower life form, such as a duck; but if you've evolved to the present as a human being, you wouldn't return to a lower form. Bad karma means you've been wicked or destructive or evil in prior lives and are trying now to pay back the debt. Any bad karma you accumulate in this life will have to be faced either in between future lives or in lives you have yet to experience — but as a human being, not a duck."

"I stand corrected. Tell me something, though. What is it you find so encouraging about all that?"

"It guarantees that we all progress, one way or another. Now you tell me something. What is it that you don't like about it?"

"Well, I guess I'm not as convinced as you are that the world is gloriously swimming onward and upward. Especially after the almost-late and not-very-much-lamented twentieth century. I grant you that our Victorian ancestors were big on progress; but it seems to me it's taken a drubbing since their time."

"I'm talking about *spiritual* progress."

"Even worse. I should think you'd have a hard time selling the notion of spiritual progress to six million Jews, or to a couple of hundred thousand Japanese at Hiroshima and Nagasaki — not to mention the unspecified number of South Americans who were tortured to death in prison. To me, it's like trying to sell someone a future lollipop in order to take her mind off a present horror she didn't deserve. It's not spiritual progress at all; it's injustice papered over by bookkeeping."

"But maybe she deserved the horror for something she did in a past life. And after she gets through it, she'll get another life that isn't a horror. So it *is* progress."

"Yes — if you buy the system. I never said reincarnation wasn't self-consistent. It is; and you can give me a perfectly respectable answer to any question I might raise about it. But look. Since you already know I have reservations, how about having me try to explain what they are?"

"Well, you're not as bad on this subject as you were on food, so go ahead. At least you're unpredictable."

"Okay. My biggest reservation is what I just said: I don't see reincarnation as any kind of truly human progress at all, spiritual or otherwise. If you take it in the strictest Oriental sense, the end of the whole process is absorption into the undifferentiated One, into Nirvana. And that's simply the end of your distinctiveness as an individual — of what you've spent your whole life, or all your lives, working on night and day. Now I grant you that individuality is pretty much a Western idea. But I happen to think it's a rather good Western idea; and I also happen to think that when Western minds — especially American Western minds — latch onto reincarnation, they very often just slap onto it the idea of progress — another Western idea — even though it doesn't really fit. Shirley MacLaine, for instance: she has too much Christian optimism to be a genuine subscriber to reincarnation."

"Have you read her?"

"Yes. And for my money, she's picked up the worst kind of Christian optimism to slap on it — the kind that's based on a very old tendency among Christians to view individual human perfection as a matter of getting certain things right. Usually, those things are certain ideas, certain essentially philosophical notions. They go by the name of *gnosticism* — the Greek notion that the universe

150

is run according to a recipe, and that the recipe, if only you can get it right, will enable you to turn yourself into a perfect soufflé. Actually, it's not a Christian notion at all; but Christians have always been sitting ducks for it because it's easier to swallow than the totally weird version of perfection presented in the Gospel."

"And what might that be?"

"That whatever perfection we're going to get will be a free gift — the gift of a whole new order — a *New Creation*. As I see it, even if reincarnation is true, it's just one more tired piece of the old order of the world. Karma is a perfect instance. As Western minds pick it up, it's simply the same old system of bookkeeping the world has always used to define perfection: somebody, or something, is always watching you, proctoring you at tests you have to keep taking over and over until you get them right — or until you flunk out completely."

"But isn't that what Christianity says? Isn't that what heaven and hell are all about?"

"No. It's what gnostic versions of heaven and hell are all about. And it's what bad Christian versions of heaven and hell have been about — like the medieval version. But it isn't what Gospel Christianity is about. In the Gospel, all such bookkeeping and scorekeeping are simply trashed in favor of the free acceptance of everybody and everything by *grace*. Nobody has to pass a single test. God is not the infinite Watchbird. Instead, he becomes incarnate in the whole, slimy, messed-up world; and his last word on the mess is simply to shut up about it in the death of Jesus and offer us a New Creation in his resurrection. The old order is simply bad news. And it's bad news because nobody can pass the tests it keeps imposing. In the New Creation there just aren't any tests. Everybody's home free."

"But reincarnation says the same thing. Eventually, everybody gets there."

"Yes. As I said, it's self-consistent; but at the price of handing out the bad news that nobody's there *yet*. The Gospel says we're all there *already*, if only we'll trust the Good News. It doesn't invite us to buy a mystique of improvement that can't be demonstrated and that allows no *present relevance* to the real sufferings of the nine-tenths of the world that's broken and smashed — like people who have turned into vegetables, and children with an I.Q. of four, and folks who are permanently psychotic. Reincarnation just makes punishments out of evils like those and waltzes around their awfulness with bookkeeping. The Gospel, on the other hand, makes the bizarre promise that it's precisely in the evil, *right smack in the present injustice,* that God bestows the healing, makes the New Creation. Our brokenness — which is where we really are, and what we really are — is actually the place of our restoration, not just a glitch on the way to it or a punishment for not getting it right. The Gospel, you see, neither calls evil insignificant nor says it's good in and of itself. It freely admits that the brokenness of the world stinks. But it does say that God meets us in our brokenness, and that by taking it all down into his own death and resurrection, he creates a New Order in which evil has no place at all."

"But you're back at the fairy tale again: the resurrection."

"As I said, if you want to call it a fairy tale, you're free to do so. But, by the same token, I can still call reincarnation a fairy tale. Once again, neither of them can be proved; but then, neither of them can be disproved, or proved impossible. What you and I are arguing about here — at least what I'm arguing about — is not whether any of this is true; it's which fairy tale is the more cheerful, the more fully human story. My biggest objection to the preoccupation with reincarnation, or past lives, or karma, is that it's all sold as part of a system, a set of laws that work just because they're laws. But I can't *love* laws: I can't love gravity, or electromagnetism, or the weak force, or the strong force — let alone the penal code or the tax code. I may admire them, or be intrigued by them, or even make a buck off them; but since they don't love me, I'm not about to love them. But the God who dies for me in Jesus — and who dies with me in my death, and who tells me the outlandish

152

Good News that I'm accepted free for nothing right in the midst of my brokenness — that's somebody I can love. Karma, at least the way Americans thump the tub for it, is loveless. Something like it is probably true, and probably has always been true: 'the sins of the fathers are visited on the children, even to the third and fourth generation.' But that's a truth of the old order; and it's a truth of which the old order has been dying for as long as we've known it. It's *bad news*. It's not part of the solution; it's the problem itself. And what God says in Jesus is that he's junked that whole order in which bookkeeping was king and made a new one in which forgiveness reigns supreme. The books have all been nailed to the cross and lost in his death. And that's the best news this old world has ever heard. Not only can I love somebody who tells me that; I can even *like* him. But I'm running on. Your turn."

"Well, I must say you're forceful and enthusiastic. But what you say doesn't sound a whole lot like what I've heard Christians say. You're a strange mix of liberal and dogmatic all at once."

"The dogmatic part is because the Gospel is about something very definite. And the liberal part is because that something is freedom — liberation from the boring old order of tit for tat."

"I like the liberal part better. But go back. A couple of times you practically admitted that reincarnation could be true. Do you really believe that, or were you just lowering your price to make a sale?"

"Strictly speaking, neither. I simply don't know whether reincarnation is a fact or not. And once again, since no person who's actually in charge of the process has ever promised me it's a fact, I can't *believe* in it, either. We're back at the old believe/know problem again: just as I can only love a *person*, I can only believe a *person*. But if you ask me what I *think* about reincarnation, I have a theory I can give you. Care to hear it?"

"Why not? You may be weird; but you're no weirder than most of the people I meet at cocktail parties — and you're a lot less weird than the food at this one."

"What I think is that reincarnation as such may not be a fact, but that the prevalence of the idea in so many cultures is the result of people picking up something that is a fact — or, to say it carefully, something *I believe to be a fact* on the basis of God's Word. What's happened, though, is that the fact hasn't been picked up by the right handle."

"And you're going to tell me both the fact and the handle, right?"

"Right. This is going to involve some shorthand, but bear with me. I believe that what God revealed in Jesus was his Incarnation in the whole world. And I believe that the Incarnation works in two ways: not only is God in the world; the world is also in God. It's his Mystical Body, so he's in it and it's in him. Now a lot of Christians think that only the church should be called the Mystical Body of God in Christ. But that's wrong. To say that only the church is the locus of the Mystery of Christ — and that the world is therefore devoid of that Mystery — is dead against the New Testament. That just makes the church a club for Christians. But the church isn't a Christian club, it's a *catholic* sign — a *sacrament* of what God has done for the *whole world*.

"So . . . trust me, I'm rounding the bend . . . if the whole world is the Mystical Body, then all of us — whether we're dead or alive, whether we're standing in the same room or living in Pittsburgh and San Diego in two different centuries — always coinhere in each other: we're always *in communion with each other*. My theory, therefore, is that maybe your past life as the widow of a Gypsy king wasn't a past life of your own, but a present reality in which you happen, by the exchanges of the Mystical Body, to be particularly involved with that woman. Those exchanges could be simply 'accidents' of the Mystical Body, just as your standing at this piano with me is one of the 'accidents' of this cocktail party. Or they could involve some deep bond between you and her — a bond so deep that you've borne her burdens and practically lived her life with her. It doesn't matter which. All that counts is that you and she are together — that you mutually *coinhere* in each other.

"Now, obviously, if it's the second kind of bond — the closest possible kind — you could easily image it to yourself in terms of a past life of your own rather than as a close relationship with somebody else. But it's also at least possible that it's a matter of a relationship and not just a case of two stages in your own identity. Anyway, end of theory."

"Well, that certainly is different. But I just don't know . . ."

"Neither do I. In the long run, it's just an idea."

"One last question, and then I really should circulate a little. Where do you stand on astrology?"

"I have no problems with it. As a matter of fact, I live with it: my wife Valerie is a professional astrologer."

"And a Christian?"

"Very much so. She's the one you ought to talk to about astrology, though. I just sort of breathe it in across the dinner table."

"You don't think it's a lot of nonsense?"

"Nope. I don't like to hear it used as fortune-telling or as an excuse for fatalism; but Valerie, thank God, never peddles it that way. For her, astrological readings are just like meteorological readings: they can tell you what the stellar and planetary weather is going to be, but it's still up to you to decide whether you sit inside and mope about the snowstorm or go out and play in it."

"You don't think it's non-Christian?"

"No — subject to the same warning about fatalism. Even Christian kings used to have court astrologers to clue them in on the 'weather.' But not to hold you up. It's been fun talking to you."

"Likewise. Give me a straight answer, though: do you think astrology is true?"

"Pretty much. But then, living with Valerie, I wouldn't dare say anything less. See you around, Stephanie. And have a good life — or lives, as the case may be."

She moved away into the crowd, and I turned to head in the opposite direction. I ran smack into Valerie.

"How long have you been standing there?" I asked.

"Oh, ever since Thelma shoved you and Stephanie together. She nailed me next, and since she never found anybody to pair me up with, I was stuck with her."

"Did you catch any of the conversation?"

"I tuned out when I heard you start in on your anti-vegetarian routine. But when you got into reincarnation, I went into warp drive and heard it all. Thelma isn't exactly a demanding conversation partner: all she needs is a human wall to bounce her voice off. I just stood in front of her and left her behind."

"Well, let's blow this pop stand and head for home. Who's driving?"

"Me. I can drive and talk at the same time; you can't. And believe me, I have plenty to say."

TEN

The Mystery and Reincarnation

For better or worse, "the group" isn't going to be canvased for their reactions to what you just overheard. Valerie, my in-house overhearer, got in ahead of them: she started in even before she'd pulled the car away from the curb.

VALERIE: I must say, you still have a knack for digging up the blondes.

ROBERT: Blame Thelma, not me. Anyway, Stephanie wasn't exactly a blonde blonde, and the mix-but-not-match getup she had on was too downtown for my taste. Not to worry.

VALERIE: I didn't. The minute I heard she was a vegetarian, I knew she'd never make your list.

ROBERT: Well, that's one item off the agenda. What's next?

VALERIE: Shirley MacLaine. You gave her too much credit for being a Christian. Anybody who meditates on the beach and says,

"I am God" over and over has a pretty big Christian wheel missing.

ROBERT: Oh, you mean my remark about her having too much Christian optimism. I thought I covered myself on that by adding that she had the worst kind of Christian optimism — the gnostic kind.

VALERIE: You've got to be a lot clearer than that with people like Stephanie. You may know that gnosticism is a recipe and Christianity isn't; but for them even the Gospel is a recipe. In their minds, all religions are just variations of one basic tapioca pudding called "spirituality." I'm surprised you didn't give her your pitch about Christianity not being a religion.

ROBERT: I started out in that direction when I was comparing vegetarianism with religions and churches. Unfortunately, though, she booted the conversation into her New Age enthusiasms, and I never got to it.

VALERIE: You could easily have picked up on it with Shirley Mac-Laine. Consciously, she's in rebellion against what I've always thought of as an Irish Roman Catholic background; but unconsciously, she's still knee-deep in the religiosity of it all. She still thinks there's something *she* has to do — like saying, "I am God," or whatever — in order to be in tune with the universe. The idea that her in-tuneness is already a fact as a result of somebody else's free gift has never occurred to her. She's too busy being in charge to let it into her mind. That's the biggest problem with a lot of New Age types, you know: they don't need God or Jesus to forgive them or offer them resurrection because they assume they can do it all themselves.

ROBERT: But I still think it's Christian gnosticism that lies at the root of the problem. They go right on assuming that the universe is run by a system rather than a lover — just like all the Christians who rattle on about the immortality of the soul as if it were the central article of the faith. For them, it's not the love of God in Christ that brings them home; it's the natural upward drift of the *real them* — their soul — that does the trick. That, plus their own mastery of the upward-drift gnosis. The trouble is, the poor old human body takes a drubbing in the process: it becomes either a disposable cocoon for the imperishable butterfly of their soul or a succession of interchangeable motels they've stayed in along the way.

VALERIE: I want to get back to the me-me-me business of having to be in charge. What reincarnation does for a lot of the people who believe in it is give them a sense of control. They don't need Jesus because even if they make a mess of the life they happen to be in, when they find themselves in between lives, *they'll* be the ones who'll decide whether they'll come back or whether they'll just stay put on the level of the spiral staircase their spiritual progress toward the One has brought them to.

ROBERT: Is that true? They really think they don't have to come back unless *they* decide?

VALERIE: Yes. And it gets worse. If, for instance, they committed suicide in one of their past lives and then decided to come back and address that, they'd be signing on for life circumstances in which suicide would be even more desirable.

ROBERT: Talk about the bad news of bookkeeping! I was right: the New Age turns out to be nothing but the old order of test-passing inflated into a metaphysical principle. You'd think that if people like Stephanie took one good look at it, they'd see that. Not only is it bad news, but all the important life-decisions it postulates take place in some never-never land no one remembers a thing about. Everything that matters occurs offstage: the actual *play* of history doesn't count except as credit or debit entries in a metaphysical ledger. It's the ledger that's reality for them; the actual world of matter, they dismiss with a wave of the hand.

VALERIE: I go back to what I said before: it's all so self-centered, and it's that way because of the need to control. Life in this world is basically out of my control. But that's a terrifying thing to recognize because it puts me in a double bind. On the one hand, the world tells me every day that I'm not the master of my fate: grandchildren develop psychological problems I wasn't even consulted about; friends lean all over me; my husband has sexy conversations with blondes. But, on the other hand, all of my training from infancy on up has been one long process of beating *responsibility* into me — of making my first response to everything that happens to me a panic reaction: "What did I do wrong? Where did I lose control? How can I get it back so I can think well of myself again?" In other words, "How can I get rid of my guilt?" So when somebody hands me a system by which I can get control over my guilt, I go for it like a dog for raw meat. And it doesn't matter what the system is, as long as it's not real Christianity. Anything else will do: medieval visions of heaven and hell; reincarnation; the working out of my karma; doing penance for my sins. Just don't try to sell me a God who says my guilt doesn't matter because she's dropped the subject. I'll give you credit on that: you came down hard on God not being the infinite Watchbird. But as you said, that's so weird to people like Stephanie that the only conclusion they can draw is not that they're being told Good News but that you're crazy.

160

ROBERT: It's an occupational hazard: Jesus had the same problem. The world is so convinced that standing on its head is the only way to go that when somebody walks in standing on his feet, it thinks he's the one who's upside down. Not that I'm not as self-centered as the next guy . . .

VALERIE: Right on!

ROBERT: . . . or the nearest gal, I might add. But it's still hard for me to see why the Good News that even our self-centeredness won't be held against us isn't met with loud hurrahs. Why does it always get the same face people pull when you mention castor oil?

VALERIE: Nobody takes castor oil anymore.

ROBERT: Okay . . . the same face they'd pull if you condemned them to an eternity of watching car-salesman commercials with no fast forward.

VALERIE: Better.

ROBERT: Seriously, though, I go back to what I said, both to Stephanie and to you here in the car: it's all so *loveless!* Maybe that's because it disguises self-centeredness as a spiritual principle. But whatever the reason is, it sure as hell makes for a cold view of life.

VALERIE: Yes. I think you almost got her with your theory about everyone coinhering in the Mystical Body — at least it got her to think that maybe reincarnation isn't the only way to pick up what people usually think of as past lives. I'm surprised you didn't put her on to Charles Williams. Mystical stuff is the best door into minds like hers — and mine too, for that matter.

ROBERT: I thought of Williams — and Julian of Norwich as well; but again, they just didn't get in: she wanted to circulate. If she ever does talk to you, maybe you could work them into the conversation. There's no guarantee, of course, that she couldn't turn them both into closet Buddhists. But it's worth a try.

VALERIE: It certainly is. I'm a closet Buddhist myself. But I agree with you: somehow she has to see the lovelessness of it all — and she has to be able to love herself, to love the life she has right now. What I think, though, is that *nobody* can do any of that unless they want to love Jesus first. Stephanie's still in love with a system that promises to make everything come out right. Until she knows that somebody loves her even though everything about her may come out wrong, it's just too much to expect that she'll let go of the system. It's too frightening to let that much freedom into your life.

ROBERT: Well! That's almost another compliment! Do I get good marks for anything else?

VALERIE: What? You're keeping score?

ROBERT: *Touché.*

VALERIE: Well, I did like the way you let her call the resurrection a fairy tale and then insisted reincarnation was in the same category. That's your old trick of pulling a punch they expect you to throw and then hitting them with one they don't expect. As I said, it's a very sexy technique: a theological submission-dominance game.

ROBERT: Anything else?

162

VALERIE: My, my. Robert is a real sponge for praise tonight, isn't he? Well, I also liked the compliment you paid *me* when you said I didn't use astrology as fatalism or a set of preordained absolutes. I like to hear my husband say nice things about me, especially if he's talking to a blonde and doesn't know I'm listening behind his back. Thank you.

ROBERT: As one sponge to another, you're welcome. And look at that — perfect timing: here we are in our own driveway!

VALERIE: It's still early. You want to watch TV?

ROBERT: What have you got in the barrel?

VALERIE: I taped this week's *Law and Order,* and we still haven't watched it.

ROBERT: Hmm. It seems I can't get away from the subject, doesn't it?

VALERIE: C'mon. You love the show — probably because you're a closet scorekeeper. Let's watch it. If you're a good boy, I'll even fast-forward the commercials.

ELEVEN

George

George was in his mid-eighties. When I first met him, some ten years ago, he was retired and not able to get around easily: he had a problem with his feet that made it difficult for him to drive a car, or even to walk short distances. Still, for as long as his wife Ursula was able to act as chauffeur, he managed to appear at church more Sundays than not and even to turn up at the occasional village art show or little theater performance. About three years ago, however, after having been in and out of the hospital a number of times, he decided it would be better if he went to a nursing home. Luckily, he found a good one, even though it was several towns removed from where he had lived. His wife visited him as often as she could; but her own health was failing, and she herself eventually became unable to drive. She died a little over a year ago.

Through it all, though, George has remained steady in his faith, active in his mind (he was a great reader until recently, but for the last few months he's been unable either to sit up in a chair or to hold a book in bed) — and a considerable talker, even under his present limitations. Visiting George has always been a pleasure for me — which is something I can't say for the general run of sick calls I've made over my forty-three years as a priest. He isn't bitter.

He isn't a complainer. He's not afraid to talk about death, and he doesn't go inert when someone else does. Best of all, he isn't a stranger to the subject of faith: his trust in God is the mainspring of his existence. I've learned more about trusting from him than he ever did from me, even though he's a fan of my books and would probably tell you he sits at my feet as far as theology is concerned.

But enough background. Once again I'm going to combine a number of conversations into a single dialogue so you can get an idea of the man. All you need to know for openers is that as I enter his room, the TV is on, and that in accordance with our usual protocol, I immediately turn it off — only to find that this time he's been listening to it through headphones.

❧   ❧

"'Morning, George."

"Father! It's good to see you. But you'll have to help me get these earphones off. My hands are even more useless than usual."

"Easily done," I said, setting them aside. "How's it going?"

"My condition hasn't exactly been pleasant lately. Sitting in a chair has been made even more difficult by the fact that I now get severe pains in the rectum every time I try to do it — and it's still impossible for me to read in bed. But I've had some good news: the doctors have decided to try something new. They've come to the conclusion that all my problems are blood-related. So they're going to 'wash' my blood — take it out, run it through some kind of filter, and run it back in again. After that, they're going to give me a program of intravenous treatments."

"Did they give you a name for this procedure?"

"Yes, but I can never remember medical terms. They've told me that it's experimental and that it may not work; but I told them to go ahead. I can accept that too, if I have to. I'm very much at peace. It's too bad they didn't think of this sooner — but then,

165

resentment is useless, and so is blame. It only makes you miserable. Most of the time, I feel fine physically and mentally, so who knows? Maybe if they can clear this up, I'll be able to begin writing the book I've talked about with you."

"The one about peace?"

"Yes. I didn't always have the peace, you know. It just came to me one day."

"I know. But you have it now, and that's what counts. Tell me something, though. I've never been clear about when the peace came to you. How long ago was it? What was going on in your life at the time?"

"I don't remember exactly when it happened — maybe it was about thirty years ago, maybe a little longer. But I do remember I was going through a very bad time. I'd been working in an unsatisfactory job, my feet were beginning to be crippled, and I had made two active suicide attempts. My life simply wasn't worth anything to me. I really must try to remember the details of that time more clearly — that's why I think writing them down would be helpful. But the important thing was very simple: one day I woke up — literally woke up in the morning — and I was at peace. I'm quite sure I hadn't done anything to achieve it. I hadn't solved any of my problems, and they certainly hadn't gone away of their own accord. I just knew in that moment that I was acceptable to God and that I could accept myself — my whole life — even though I knew I really wasn't any different from what I had been. I just stopped condemning myself for what I had been.

"But the wonderful thing was that I never seriously wondered if the peace would last. Naturally, it *occurred* to me that it might not; but since I hadn't done anything to get it, I decided that I didn't have to do anything about keeping it. It was simply a gift, and it was mine. I did think once or twice that it might be a delusion or some temporary euphoria; but I decided against that too. If anything, my life before was the delusion, and the peace was the reality. And even if it was only the result of some chemical

166

or psychological state that would come to an end and leave me back where I was, that didn't make any difference, either, because it was *what I had been* that had been accepted. It was *me,* not any changes or promised changes in my life or my actions. But I'm afraid I'm not explaining it very well. Perhaps you could explain it to me better."

"You're explaining it very well, George. But as a matter of fact, a couple of things do occur to me. The first is that what you're describing is very much like Jesus' parable of the King's Son's Wedding. You know: the one where the king invites all his worthy, high-class friends to the wedding, and they refuse to come. So what does the king do? He sends out his servants, drags in all the street people, dresses them up in proper clothes, and has the wedding party anyway. That's *acceptance* — and, just like your acceptance of the peace of God, it's an acceptance that's given without any reference to their 'worthiness.' But once it's been given, it's *their acceptance of that acceptance* that enables them to enjoy the party. Therefore, the peace you've experienced since that day thirty years ago is a peace that was always there for you simply because God always wanted to give it to you — just as the acceptance of the street people was there simply because the king wanted guests at his party. And as you clearly saw, it had no more to do with your merits or demerits than it did with theirs: it was a gift, pure and simple. Luckily, though, like most of those at the wedding party, you made a decision to accept the gift the minute you saw it. You weren't like the fellow at the end of the parable who gets kicked into outer darkness (where there is no peace) because he wouldn't accept the free wedding costume. You follow?"

"Yes. And even if for some reason I found myself outside the wedding party again — out in the darkness, with no peace — God would still be inviting me back in all the time because he really wants nothing more than to give me the gift of peace. And so the next time I found myself at peace, all I would ever have to do is accept it again, just as I did the first time."

"That's right. And that acceptance is faith: the simple act of *trusting* the one who gives you the peace. You don't even have to try to hold onto the peace, or do a lot of things that will earn you the peace. Even if you went into a depression and lost your grip on it, you could still trust Jesus and just wait patiently for your awareness of the peace he's always giving you to return. But his gift of peace would be there all along."

"I'm glad you said that. I didn't mean to imply that I've never been troubled these thirty years. But I did trust that the peace was there — and that it really didn't depend on me."

"I think you made that very clear, George. A lot clearer than it is to most people. When Christians think about Jesus giving them peace, or acceptance, or forgiveness, or whatever you want to call it, they very often picture it to themselves the wrong way. They imagine that Jesus is somewhere else — that he's not with them but apart from them. Either they think he's a character back in history or, if they believe he's God, they think he's far away in some place called 'heaven.' But in either case, they think that it's up to them to do something to *earn* his presence in their lives — and that if they don't do the right, worthy, merit-earning things, he won't be in them at all.

"Unfortunately, the church has often encouraged that kind of thinking. It may pay lip service to the truth that we're saved by faith and not by works; but in practice it acts as if only those who can manage to live right will get the gifts of God in Christ. But the New Testament has a much better way of talking about how we're saved. It talks about the gift of God — peace, forgiveness, grace, reconciliation — as a *Mystery*, as something *already present* in all of creation. But precisely because it is a Mystery, it's present in a *hidden* way. In other words, it's a gift you can only *trust* to be there, not something whose presence you can know, or prove, or work your way toward. In church we talk about this as the *Mystery of Faith*, or the *Paschal Mystery* — meaning the hidden presence of Jesus, by the power of his death and resurrection, in the whole creation. But the New Testament has a number of other names for it. Sometimes it refers to it as *the mystery of God's will;* sometimes it talks about it as the *dispensation* — the activity in the world — *of the mystery hidden for ages by the God who created all things;* sometimes it calls it *the mystery of the Gospel;* but principally it talks about it as *the mystery of Christ.*

"Now what I think the Mystery of Christ really means is that when God becomes incarnate in Jesus, he isn't just doing a job on one person who happened to live in Palestine two thousand years ago. Rather, he's manifesting in Jesus — making sacramentally present in Jesus — what he's been doing all along in all persons and, for that matter, in all things. But it's also more than that. The Incarnation isn't just God coming into the world of time and place; it's also God taking all times and places into himself so that they'll all be present to him in his peacemaking, forgiving, reconciling power. Nobody is left out, you see. But maybe I'm losing you. Am I going too fast?"

"Not at all. Go on."

"All right, then: that explains why salvation is by faith alone, and not by works. It's already there for everybody. Nobody has to run around looking for it. All they have to do is *believe* it — *trust* it, *accept that it's true already* — and they're home free. All of which is practically the same thing you said to begin with. But now I want to give you an illustration.

"You know what all this is like, George? It's like a dance — a big formal party that everybody is already invited to and present at. Now what happens at a dance? When the band starts to play, almost everybody decides to trust the 'new world' of the dance and to act accordingly: they move in harmony with the music. But when the band takes a break, they go back to acting in accordance with the 'old world' they know better: husbands and wives get into arguments; some people drink too much; others try to make real-estate deals; and so on.

"If you think about that, it gives you a much better picture

169

of what Christians are really supposed to be up to. Because the dance that God has invited us to — the dance of the Mystery of Christ — is always going on: the band playing the music of forgiveness never takes a break. The music of the Mystery, of course, is *hidden* music: we have to *trust* that it's being played — and for anyone who doesn't trust, it's just as if there's no music going on at all. Christians, therefore, are not some select group who have music nobody else has; they're simply people who by faith — by trust — always hear the music of the Mystery of Christ that the whole creation has been provided with. And so the real job of Christians as far as the world is concerned is simply to dance to the hidden music — and to try, by the joy of their dancing, to wake the world up to the party it's already at, even though it thinks it doesn't hear any music at all."

"It's been more than thirty years since I could dance," George said. "But I see your point: the peace is a kind of dancing to the music, even if I can't move at all."

"Exactly. T. S. Eliot called the cross — the death of Christ — 'the still point of the turning world'; and except for that point, he said, 'there would be no dance.' That was in the *Four Quartets*. And somewhere else in them he says, 'So the darkness shall be the light, and the stillness the dancing.' It's only when we can sit still in our deaths — present 'deaths,' like your inability to hold a book, or our final death in death itself — that we can hear the music at all. Everything else we might do is just noise that drowns it out. It's only when we listen in the stillness that grace can have its way with us. But grace is always there because Jesus is always there: any time we stop our noise, the music comes up."

George thought about that for a while. "Somehow," he said, "I'm reminded of Bonhoeffer. I read his book called *The Cost of Discipleship* — the one in which he makes a distinction between 'cheap grace' and 'costly grace.' I'm not a disciple, of course. I'm just trying to be a Christian. Bonhoeffer was a real disciple. What do you think of him?"

"Well, George, I've always had a problem with the phrase 'cheap grace.' As far as I'm concerned, nobody can make God's grace in Jesus any cheaper than it already is: it's *free*. I suppose if a person *thinks* he has to do something to earn it or buy it, and then does less than that, you might say he's cheapened grace. But since he was wrong to start with — since it wasn't really grace he was dealing with, but only a false notion of it in his own head — he hasn't even gotten close to the subject, let alone 'cheapened' it. But what I really object to is people who use the so-called danger of cheap grace as a way of browbeating others into thinking there's some level of performance they have to achieve before they can be worthy of grace.

"Look at what you just said. You said you weren't a disciple in Bonhoeffer's league, just someone trying to be a Christian. I don't buy that. I think your acceptance of all your difficulties *is* discipleship. And since it's always easier *not* to accept such things — to resent them, and to blame other people or God for them — I suppose that in some sense it's true that you've made the 'costly' response to grace, and that those who wallow in resentment and blame have made the 'cheap' response. But the distinction still bothers me because it leads someone like you — someone who really sees that the peace that comes by grace is the only thing that matters, the only thing God finally cares about — to say you're somehow not doing what you obviously are doing.

"I guess what I really don't like is the way people start out by defining sin as 'moral failure' and then go on to think that if they commit 'sins' they'll cut themselves off from grace. That's all nonsense, of course: 'sinners' are the very thing God gives his grace to — lost sheep, lost coins, lost sons. As a matter of fact, the true New Testament opposite of sin isn't virtue, or moral success, or getting your act together: it's faith in the grace that takes away all the sins of the world. Paul says, 'All that is not of faith is sin.' And Jesus says, 'The one who believes is not judged.' We're not on trial: 'There is therefore now no condemnation for those who are in

Christ Jesus.' And we shouldn't weaken that by giving a narrow interpretation to 'those who are in Christ Jesus': the whole world is in him, reconciled and made into a New Creation by the Mystery of Christ."

George thought some more. "I don't know. It sounds very much like 'Shall we continue in sin, that grace may abound?' When Paul thought of that, he said, 'God forbid!'"

"He didn't say 'God forbid!' George; he said *me genoito,* which literally means 'Let it not happen' — but which I think means something more like 'No way!' or 'Nonsense!' Because it *is* nonsense. Grace abounds no matter what we do about our 'sins.' We can't make it abound any more than it does, either by committing sins or by not committing them. It simply takes away *all* sins, regardless; the only thing we have to do is trust it."

"Well," he said, "I suppose you're right. That certainly was true for Ursula. I talked to her on the telephone every day the last time she was in the hospital — even an hour before she died. In spite of everything that was wrong with her, she had real faith. I was very happy for her at the end."

"I know that, George. I took her Communion the day before she died, and we talked about receiving Communion and saying the Lord's Prayer as acts of faith. She was very much at peace. And, speaking of which, I brought the Sacrament with me. Would you like to receive now?"

He said, "Yes, I would."

When Communion was over, he was quiet. "You know," he said, "I'm content to make the most I can of my life, whatever that may be. I'm at peace."

"I know you are, George. We all are, even those who don't believe it. We all have two lives: the one we have right now, which is wearing down and will eventually end in death; and the one we have in Jesus, which will never wear out. Making the most of the life you have now is important because that's the life God has taken into himself in Jesus. But the really important thing is the life of Jesus that you and I and everyone has in us. That's the life that will make the most of *us,* no matter what we do. Everything is safe. All we need to do is trust him. I'll see you in a couple of weeks, okay? By then, maybe you'll have something to report about the blood procedure."

"I hope so," he said. "We'll see."

TWELVE

The Mystery and Faith

ROBERT: That visit with George is the last conversation I'm going to give you in this book, so why don't we talk about your reactions to him for a while and then head for the barn? You can ask any other questions you like, of course, but eventually I do want to make one final pass at tying up what I've been trying to say about the Mystery of Christ. Who's first?

LOUISE: I liked George — and you seemed to, too. I think you were different with him than with most of the others — more relaxed, not so aggressive. Maybe his "peace" rubbed off on you. Tell me, though: did they ever do that blood-filtering procedure on him? It sounded very strange to me.

ROBERT: No, they didn't, Louise. The doctors finally decided it wasn't necessary and treated him instead with injections of something he called immunoglobulin. Whatever it was, it's worked wonders. I visited him again just two weeks ago, and he was sitting up with no discomfort at all. Not only that, but he's paying a woman to come in three days a week and help him with his book. She's got all his papers in order, and she's willing to take any dictation he wants to give her. He and I talked a bit about how to use her time to advantage. Since he still can't write or hold a book (and therefore can't make notes to dictate from), I suggested he try dictating his notes first and have her type them up. Then, after he's got those in order, he could try dictating a chapter and see how it goes. One of his sons is making him a lap tray to solve the book-and-paper-holding problem, so he's enthusiastic about taking a crack at his project. He's a remarkable guy.

OTTO: He certainly is. Do you know the name of the ailment he's suffering from?

ROBERT: Neuropathy is what he called it, but I really don't know anything more about it. George says the doctors are pleased with his progress, though, and feel they're on the right track.

ENID: I think that's wonderful. I only hope I can be half as positive if I ever find myself in circumstances like that. But if I may, I'd like to go back for a minute to something Louise said. You really were different with George, Robert; but I think the difference may be rooted in something that has more to do with you than with him. For whatever reason, you seem generally to be less aggressive — or less confrontational — with the men in this book than with the women. Perhaps that's because of your theological exasperation with the problems they presented and has nothing to do with the sex of the persons involved. But I don't think so: Dan was a theological pain in the neck, but you were more laid back with him than you were with, say, Mabel. I think there's a lot of male-sun-sign energy hovering around you, and that you're just more comfortable with men. You're polite with women, of course; and with all three of the women we've met, you even blended your politeness with flirtatious-ness. But it seems to me the flirting is a shield you put up against your unease with female energy. What is your sun sign, anyway?

175

ROBERT: Libra.

ENID: See? I was right! That's definitely a male sign.

ROBERT: I plead guilty — but with an explanation. My moon is in Capricorn and my ascendant is Cancer, so I'm not totally devoid of female energy.

ENID: There's nothing to be guilty about: on balance, I think you're quite fair. But I felt the energy, so I thought I'd mention it.

ROBERT: It's been mentioned before — by experts, resident and otherwise. As a matter of fact, I've also been accused of having unresolved mother-issues and of seeking the company of women as a cover-up for not having dealt with them. I'd like to be able to tell you I was cured, or even in recovery, but that's not for me to say. So, please! Somebody get us back to George.

LOUISE: Well, I liked the way you filled us in on his progress just now. But it made me wonder. Way back somewhere, you said that Helen might show up again in this book. I'd love to hear what happened to her.

ROBERT: Unfortunately, Louise, she hasn't been back for another visit. I see her often enough on public occasions, but she's never brought up the subject of what she decided to do about her affair.

LOUISE: You never asked?

ROBERT: No. That's her business; I don't need to know about it unless she decides she wants to talk about it again. I don't think it's useful for a priest to barge in on counselees and try

176

to move them faster than they're prepared to go. Helen has to have a reason of her own for coming to me. She obviously did the first time around. If she ever finds another one, there'll be a second time; if not, not.

LOUISE: But you're not curious?

ROBERT: Yes. But not enough to try to gratify my curiosity by wheedling information out of her — or out of anyone else who might be able to tell me, for that matter. Until *she* makes it my business, it isn't.

LOUISE: That must be hard — I mean, not knowing what happened to people who invited you into their lives.

ROBERT: It goes with the territory, Louise. There are three possibilities in a situation like this. One, she was satisfied with what I told her — namely, that in Jesus there's no condemnation for any of her decisions, even if they're "bad" ones — and because of that, she finds herself able to live with whatever decision she's made. Two, she was dissatisfied with my counseling and has no intention of ever subjecting herself to the experience again. Or three, she's still pretty much where she was when she first came to me and has nothing new to report. But whatever the case, I've done what I could, given my opportunities, talents, and limitations. I should be content to wait.

ALICE: But maybe she *expects* you to follow up.

ROBERT: Second-guessing other people's unexpressed expectations is not a good basis for action. Look. Counseling is no different from preaching as far as a priest is concerned. People come to ask for advice or to hear sermons for more reasons than there are dandelions in my lawn. Some of them come to learn, some to have their egos massaged, some to have their prejudices confirmed, and some to get the church to take over responsibility for their lives. But those reasons are all irrelevant to me as a counselor or a preacher. What I have to deal with is *persons,* not motives. It's the warm bodies sitting in front of me that I'm called to minister to. And with whatever skills or disabilities I possess, my job is only to preach the Gospel, the Good News, to them, "whether they will hear, or whether they will forbear." Furthermore, even when I've done that, Jesus tells me I'm supposed to say, "I'm an unprofitable servant; I've only done what it was my duty to do." So if that's enough for him, it should be enough for me. That's why I've never in my whole life thanked anybody who complimented me on either my advice or my preaching. All I ever say to them is "Good!" and let it go at that. If they tell me what I said was terrific, *that's* good; if they tell me it was awful — well, that's good too: at least they spotted it. But enough of that. Let's move on.

FRANK: I have a question for you. To me, some of the things George said didn't sound as specifically Christian as you seemed to think they were. His understanding of God was a bit generalized and philosophical for me — not particularly nailed down to Jesus as the only Lord and Savior. There was one point, in fact, where he sounded pretty much like a universalist — saying that even if he found himself in the outer darkness, with no peace, God would still be inviting him back in again all the time. That struck me as playing kind of fast and loose with the parable of the King's Son's Wedding — not to mention the other places in God's Word where Jesus himself says hell is eternal: ". . . where their worm dieth not, and the fire is not quenched." And what about "the second death" in the Book of Revelation?

ROBERT: We've been over some of that ground before, Frank, and I think you know where I stand on it. For my money, you can't resolve the question of whether hell is eternal just by quoting spot passages. You have to start with the truth that Jesus, in his death and resurrection, has taken away *all* the sins of the world: there is absolutely nothing and no one — either now or at the last day — who isn't being presented to the Father as clean as a whistle by Jesus. Of course, if there are some of us at the last day who want to argue with that and tell God we like our old, nonexistent version of ourselves better than his repair job on us in Jesus — well, at that point we can go to hell. But it's only our non-acceptance of God's acceptance that can get us there, not our sins.

And as to whether even people who take that attitude have to *stay* in hell, I don't think we should be too quick to answer Yes. After all (to spot a passage in Revelation myself), Jesus says, "Behold, I stand at the door and knock" — which, since the verb "stand" is in the present tense, seems to mean that as the result of his saving action, his knocking at our door with forgiveness is not just an invitation he extended to us once, but one he *always extends* in every present moment. Maybe the "hell" of hell is the eternal racket of his knocking as it beats on the ears of those who wish he'd just go away and leave them alone.

And as to whether George's faith was too generalized, I don't think that's an important question to answer at all. We aren't saved by passing theology tests. George is baptized, he receives Communion gladly and willingly, and he believes God has given him peace. Sure, I too would like it better if his theological observations were a little more tightly focused on Jesus. But the real point is that Jesus is tightly focused on George, and that however George formulates his faith (and he does — all you have to do is listen to him), it's his *faith* he's formulating, and *that's* probably just fine with Jesus. The

Mystery of Christ is operative in us whether we know it or not, or whether we get a proper intellectual handle on it or not. The power of Jesus' death and resurrection makes a New Creation of the whole world; after that, any response we may make to it is distinctly secondary — and if that response is an inconvenience to anybody, at most it's only an inconvenience to ourselves.

OTTO: All right; but that brings up something that's been bothering me all along. You say the Mystery of Christ — the New Creation in Jesus — works in and by the death and resurrection of Jesus. What I want to know is . . .

ROBERT: I have to stop you right there, Otto. I was dealing with George in real life, so I didn't balk at his imprecise formulations. But this is a theological discussion — an intellectual game — and focus is one of the rules of the game here. Be precise. The Mystery of Christ works *everywhere* in the universe, not just in the death and resurrection of Jesus. True enough, it was manifested finally, fully, really, and sacramentally in the death and resurrection of Jesus, but its operation is not limited to those acts, nor is it dependent on anyone's getting a proper hookup to them: Jesus is not the Lighting Company of the world.

OTTO: I understand that. But that's precisely what leads to my question. What I want to know is, How necessary is it to your view of the Mystery of Christ for Jesus literally to have risen from the dead? There are an awful lot of modern people who have a hard time accepting as historically true something like the resurrection of a person who lived two thousand years ago, when the communal mind-set was amenable to such stuff. Nowadays, things are different. I mean, really: how many present-day Christians do you think actually believe, for example, that Jesus literally sailed up into a cloud at the ascension?

ROBERT: To be honest with you, Otto, some do and some don't. But to be accurate with you as well, it seems to me you're talking about people who were "modern" some fifty or sixty years ago, when you and I were thinking these things through for the first time. *That* modern world was still very much enamored of a "scientific," non-miraculous universe which, for all its up-to-dateness back in those days, was pretty much a dead ringer for the old, eighteenth-century, deistic universe. But the intellectual world we live in today isn't so sure that inexplicable phenomena can't happen. It's a bit more open to the charm of systems that are not so philosophically law-ridden. And as far as the popular imagination nowadays is concerned . . . well, think of Stephanie: if someone can swallow reincarnation, how much of a strain can it be to accept resurrection?

OTTO: That's as it may be. I've heard you do that number before, particularly on the resurrection and the ascension. You claim there are only two possible theological choices about those matters: either we accept as historical fact the assertion that Jesus revealed the Mystery of Christ by literally rising from the dead and then taking off from a mountaintop, or we have to admit that the early church made up the stories out of whole cloth. But I think that's a choice between two straw men. Look. You're talking about the revelation of a cosmic mystery, right? — about a New Creation that's the work of the Incarnate Word of God. Well, it seems to me that since *no particular way* of revealing that mystery will ever render it accessible except by faith, *any* way of getting it revealed will pass muster. It doesn't much matter to me whether Jesus acted it out or the early church cooked it up. In either case, the revelation would still come through a set of circumstances *sanctioned by the Holy Spirit* — through "historical" circumstances or "mythical" circumstances, as the case may be. Why do you feel the "historical circumstance" approach is the only valid one? You certainly make allowances for myth in other places — as in the Adam and Eve narrative in Genesis. Why can't you allow myth when it comes to the resurrection and the ascension? Aren't there a lot of twentieth-century theologians who find that perfectly acceptable?

ROBERT: Yes, there are. Bultmann is the name that comes immediately to mind; but there have been plenty more since his time, and even a fair number before him. And incidentally, Otto, you did a rather good job of putting the best possible face on their position — especially in what you said about the Holy Spirit being able to use either historical or mythical circumstances to get the job of revealing the Mystery done. But before I get to that, let me spend a little time explaining for everybody else's benefit just how modern theologians handle the "myth" approach in the case of the resurrection of Jesus.

OTTO: Haven't we been over that before? I seem to remember your suggesting that the Adam and Eve story might best be taken as a "myth" — provided we understand that while a particular "myth" may be an imaginative fiction, it can also be just as valid a way of talking about what happened in the course of history as the literal enumeration of actual events. What was it you said about it? Ah! I remember — you said myth is the only way we have of talking about the significance of chapters in history that no historians were around to witness.

ROBERT: You have a good memory, Otto. But precisely because

182

the New Testament claims there were indeed witnesses to Jesus' resurrection and ascension, I'd like to add a couple of refinements to my position at this point. May I?

OTTO: Be my guest.

ROBERT: Okay, here goes. When modern theologians take the "myth" approach to the resurrection of Jesus, they put a slightly different spin on it than they put on the Adam and Eve story. Rather than simply calling his rising from the dead an imaginative fiction, they refer to it as a "Christ event." By that, they mean that even though they may feel the resurrection itself didn't take place as a literal, historical event in A.D. 29, they can still hold that the experience the early church had of Christ after his death was very definitely an event in history — hence, the "Christ event." For them, in other words, what "actually happened" as far as the resurrection is concerned was not an event that occurred in a tomb in Jerusalem but one that took place in the "faith consciousness" of the early church. It happened historically, therefore; but it happened in a slightly different way than the Gospel writers seem to have assumed it did.

And those theologians opt for that interpretation because they find the New Testament evidence for a "historical" resurrection (and, even more, a "historical" ascension) less convincing than more traditional minds do. Just to give you a couple of the points they make: Paul never mentions the "empty tomb"; Luke seems to assign the ascension to both the evening of Easter Day (in the Gospel) and to forty days after (in the Book of Acts); and Paul assumes that his vision of the risen Jesus on the road to Damascus has exactly the same status as the other apostles' sightings of him on the first Easter and the days following (though I think Paul clearly assumes that those earlier appearances were historical events).

OTTO: Hmm. I thought you took a dim view of people who question the historicity of the resurrection and the ascension.

ROBERT: I don't take a dim view of such people, Otto; I just think that these particular theologians find those "negative evidences" compelling for reasons that are more philosophical than historical: I'm still of the opinion that the operative factor in their reasoning is an old-fashioned, deistic prejudice against miracles. After all, the only *historical* record we have (namely, the New Testament) claims he actually rose from the dead and ascended up in the air; any reconstruction of a "different history" behind the accounts we actually have is just conjecture that's even less provable than they are. It's put forward not because of other or better evidence but because of a philosophical predisposition to question the mind-set of those who gave us the accounts.

Furthermore, while this quest for the "history behind the history" is undertaken to provide a way around certain perceived difficulties with biblical literalism, it is itself a kind of fundamentalism: it's still a quest for some unflawed original that, because it will tell us what *really* happened, will supposedly make the leap of faith easier. But there are two things wrong with that approach. First, Christianity has never given much houseroom to the idea of an unflawed original, even in the case of Holy Scripture. In fact, the biblical records we have of Jesus are remarkably un-original. On the one hand, except for a handful of phrases, we don't have any of his words as he first spoke them in Aramaic; on the other, even the "original Greek" we do have hasn't been held to be "necessary to salvation": the New Testament has been presented *in translation* at every turn in the church's missionary enterprise. But second, even if we could arrive at some more original (and therefore more "correct") evidence of Jesus' words or of the events of his life, we would still be

184

left with the necessity of deciding whether to *believe in him* as the Incarnate Word in whom the Mystery of Christ is revealed. No evidence of any kind, whether from Scripture itself or from purportedly more reliable corrections of Scripture, can *constrain* faith.

Therefore, even if this hankering for an unflawed original could be gratified, we would still have to face the truly radical departure — the quantum leap *beyond all evidence* — that faith inevitably calls for. It would still be necessary to get past the business of mere assent to ideas about Jesus to *trust in Jesus himself* — a progress that no easing of perceived "intellectual difficulties" makes one whit less a *leap* of faith.

Still, despite the fact that the Christ-event approach seems to me to be both fundamentalistic and philosophically rather than evidentially motivated, a *theological* case of sorts can be made for it. In fact, you yourself sketched out that case quite succinctly. As you said, if the Holy Spirit is going to reveal the cosmic Mystery of Christ — of the Incarnation of the Word of God — that Mystery is going to be accessible to us only by faith, no matter how the Spirit chooses to reveal it. It can never be a matter of simple knowledge arrived at on the basis of proof that someone literally died and rose — or did any other particular thing. The resurrection is indeed the greatest of Jesus' signs; but, like all his other signs (the changing of water into wine, for example), it's readable only by those who decide to *believe* in him, not by the general run of "objective observers."

Think about that. Even if we had a videotape of the resurrection, we still wouldn't be able to prove what we believe — namely, that in Jesus' death, all deaths are made the locus of God's saving work, and that when Jesus rises, the whole world rises as a New Creation in him. Those propositions can be arrived at only on the basis of *trust in Jesus,* not evidence; they proclaim a Mystery that no fact of our experience, not

185

even the fact of Jesus' resurrection, can cause our minds to arrive at as a necessary consequence.

So whichever way the Holy Spirit decides to reveal the Mystery of Christ, we still have the problem of making the leap of faith — of getting ourselves from *mere knowledge of the signs* by which he reveals it to *belief in the Incarnate Word* whom he's revealing. If he decides to do it by having Jesus act out a *literal rising from the dead,* we still have to decide whether to believe such a resurrection is the centerpiece of God's action in history or to write it off as just another corpse revival, like the raising of Lazarus. And if he decides to make the revelation by having the early church express its faith-consciousness of Jesus as resurrection and life by putting that consciousness *in the form of a historical resurrection narrative,* we still have to decide whether to accept that "Christ event" as the work of the Holy Spirit revealing the Mystery of the love of God *in Jesus,* or to reject it as just another intriguing but still strictly human idea.

But perhaps that's enough on the "faith" aspect of the question. As far as the *theology* of it is concerned, it should be obvious by now that neither the "literal event" view nor the "Christ event" view can stand without further refinements to overcome their built-in theological shortcomings. The *literal event view,* for example, has to be stated in such a way that we don't confine the Mystery of resurrection to the events of Easter Day, or limit its effect only to persons who take the proper religious steps to get themselves hooked up to it. In other words, we have to theologize it as a *cosmic* Mystery — a *catholic* operation going on everywhere, always, and for everybody. We mustn't make it out to be just some extra burst of divine power that got plugged into the world at a specific time and place and therefore needs transmission lines before it can reach people who weren't around when it happened. Once again, we mustn't turn Jesus into the Lighting Company

186

of the world. The Mystery of Christ has been the Light of the world *all along:* it's a "mystery hidden from ages and generations" and now finally *revealed* in Jesus, not a new divine strategy designed to attract suitably select customers.

On the other hand, the *Christ-event view* has to be stated in such a way that the Mystery can't be written off as just another instance of merely human speculation; the resurrection as Christ event must be stated as nothing less than the sacrament, the real presence of *the action of God himself in history.*

Accordingly — to sum it up — if the resurrection is taken as a literal, "time and place" event, it still has to be proclaimed as the manifestation of a *catholic* Mystery, and if the resurrection is taken as a "Christ event," it still has to be proclaimed as the manifestation of a *historical* Mystery.

The trick, therefore, is to formulate *both* views correctly. Through most of this book I've been trying to correct the "literal event" view to state it in such a way that the Mystery of Christ can be seen as a cosmic fact that's true for all and not just as a transaction that's available only to some. But let me spend just a minute or so on the "Christ event" view and spell out how I would guard against *its* possible misformulations.

First of all, the "Christ event" has to be clearly stated as *the work of the Holy Spirit.* I think most modern theologians really do see it that way and not just as a product of the human mind. Unfortunately, though, some of the ways they talk about it need refining if people, particularly traditionalists, are not to be put off by it. To take just one example, it's a commonplace among modern theologians to refer to miraculous events like the literal resurrection of Jesus as "category errors." By that, they mean something like this: When people have a profound experience of a reality that's beyond anything they can put into an intelligible category, they frequently express it by putting it into a category they can make at least some sense of . . .

ALICE: I can't say that's very clear to me. Do you think you could give us an illustration?

ROBERT: Sure. Think of a person who falls deliriously in love. In order to express his inner conviction of the greatness of his love for the beloved, he may well say to her, "God made us for each other from all eternity and arranged our lives so we would meet." Now, at the very least, that's not a statement of anything the gentleman in question knows to be a fact of history. It's a theological opinion, and a questionable one at that. It assumes that God is the immediate cause of the events of history — a proposition that not even believers in divine providence necessarily subscribe to. The gentleman, in short, has made a "category error": he has substituted the category of detailed divine intervention for the category of a profound personal experience of love.

Now if you apply that to the early church's experience of the "Christ event" — of the "risen Christ" — you get at least an inkling of what modern theologians are talking about. Peter and Paul, for example, were profoundly convinced by their experience of Jesus after his death that he was the center of their lives — and that because of him, both sin and death had been conquered for them (even though both unhappy facts went right on happening before their very eyes). So, in order to express their conviction that this invisible victory was a reality (indeed, that it was and is the pivotal reality of all history), they took it out of the category of inward experience and put it into the category of literal historical event — that is, they conceived of it as an actual resurrection at a specific time and place. (A lot of modern people wouldn't do that, of course, because they don't think resurrections can really happen; but for Peter and Paul and the early church, such miracles were not necessarily any less real than rain on the roof.)

As I said, I have no objection to that approach as long as people simply take it to mean that the Holy Spirit decided to use the "category error" phenomenon as one of his many devices for revealing the historicity of the Mystery of Christ. They won't be claiming, of course, that the Spirit "made" the category error; they will simply hold (given their general point of view) that he allowed it to happen under the aegis of his inspiration because it was just another way of bringing the Mystery to our attention.

I do, however, have a lingering reservation about one possible reason why modern theologians may prefer the "Christ event" explanation of how the Holy Spirit revealed the Mystery. They seem to me to be so obsessed with the *intellectual* scandal of a literal resurrection that they imagine that, if they can only get rid of it for us, faith in the action of God in history will go down our modern throats more smoothly. But to me, that comes perilously close to attempting to do an end run around the truly monumental scandal of the Gospel itself — to implying that it can and should somehow be rendered nonscandalous. But it can't and it shouldn't be. The real scandal of the Mystery of Christ is *what* has been done in Jesus, not *how* it was revealed. What we are asked to believe at the end of *any* presentation of the modus operandi of the Mystery is the scandal of the Cross — the absurdity, the sheer *foolishness* and *weakness* (to use Paul's words) of what God incarnate in Jesus has actually gone and done. *He has died to our sins on the cross and given us a whole New Creation — which is nevertheless totally invisible to any human intellectual scrutiny.* And therefore I remain suspicious of those theologians who strain at the gnat of the intellectual difficulty of Christ's resurrection: it makes me wonder if they

189

have taken the full measure of the camel of Mystery they are actually being asked to swallow by faith.

Nevertheless — to wind up this heavy theological sledding — either of the two views (the resurrection as "literal event" or the resurrection as "Christ event") can be presented as a historical revelation of the Mystery, but both of them need theological refinement if they're not to be misconstrued. Personally, I still lean in the direction of the "literal event" interpretation. I really do think the early church first experienced the resurrection as a very odd historical event that simply perplexed the immediate followers of Jesus, but then, because of their faith in him — and, above all, as a result of their experience of the Holy Spirit at Pentecost — they came to understand and to proclaim the Mystery-laden implications of their faith. I'm not as averse as some of my contemporaries to a God who gives occasional historical "signs" (miracles). But since the "Christ event" interpretation, properly expounded, turns out to be just another historical "sign" that points beyond itself to the Mystery of Christ at the heart of history — and since the point of both interpretations is that God acts in and is the Lord of history — I'm not about to fault anyone who finds it more comfortable intellectually, even though I myself find it an elaborate way of doing what the New Testament does much more simply. It's a bit like blasting your way into the back of the empty tomb when the front door is already open. Anyway, end of sleigh ride.

ENID: Well! I'm glad *that's* over! I've been dying to get back to George. I particularly liked the little exchange you had with him after you brought up the image of the Mystery of Christ as a dance that's going on everywhere and always for everybody. I don't know if he quite picked up your point about Christians simply being the people who by faith always hear the music of that dance: he just observed that it was thirty years since he

190

could dance — though he did say his peace was a kind of dancing to the music. But what I really liked was the way you brought in Eliot's "So the stillness shall be the dancing." We need more appreciation of that. Everybody's so busy making noises about the ethical, social, and theological implications of the Mystery that they forget it really does work mostly in darkness, stillness, and silence. *That's* the main point — and it's certainly what the mystics insist on over and over.

ROBERT: Thank you, Enid. You know something? You've just turned this discussion onto a track that could lead us to the wrap-up. I think if no one has any other pressing questions, I might just try to tie together as briefly as possible all the threads of the Mystery we've dealt with in this book. Is that okay with all of you?

FRANK: Well, for a long time now I've been wanting to press you a little harder about your objection to Bonhoeffer's condemnation of "cheap grace." But if it's too late for that, we can skip it.

ROBERT: It's never too late, Frank. What did you have in mind?

FRANK: Maybe it's my evangelical upbringing, but I always get the feeling you don't take sin seriously. I mean, aren't we supposed to fight against sin? There are literally dozens of places in the New Testament — lots of them even in Paul — where the duty to forsake sin is spelled out. What do you do with those?

ROBERT: First of all, Frank, I make a distinction. I myself take sin very seriously. As far as I'm concerned, it's what messes up my life, so anything I can do to resist it will make me, and those around me, a lot happier than we presently are. However, as far as God is concerned, he does and he doesn't take sin seriously. He *does,* because he cares enough to die for our sins in the Person of his only begotten Son. But, on the other hand, having done that, he *doesn't* take our sins seriously anymore. He has taken away the "handwriting that was against us and nailed it to his cross," and so "there is therefore now no condemnation to those who are in Christ Jesus" — as I've observed several times already, in case you haven't noticed. Once again, his entire relationship with us is based on the *presumption of our innocence in Christ.*

But even if I take my sins seriously, I still have to make a further distinction between sins and Sin. I can, at certain times and in certain departments, manage to stop committing *sins* with a small *s;* but there's no way I myself can ever do anything about overcoming *Sin* with a capital *S.* Only God can do that. *Sin* is the inveterate tendency of human beings to serve themselves rather than God, or their neighbors, or the creation God gave them. Even my efforts to get rid of it will inevitably — somewhere, somehow — be tainted by self-serving. I can corrupt any act, however good: I can tell you the truth, for example, in order to hurt you or get even with you. Sin is not just "bad action"; it's a condition of *all the actions* of the fallen human race. That's not to say, of course, that we never do anything good. But it is to say that our actions are never going to be able to bring about the ultimate triumph of goodness over evil. Only *grace* can achieve that, not any works on our part.

That's why I think the phrase "cheap grace" is inevitably misleading. Grace gives us total restoration as an utterly free gift; we already have it, so all we have to do, and all we can possibly do, to enjoy it is *believe* we have it. But to go on from that point and say that there's a "costly" response to grace that's better than some supposed "cheap" one seems to me to take away the sovereignty of salvation by grace alone, through faith. The fallen world already imposes enough invidious divisions on us; we don't need to add another one that sorts us into spiritual hotshots who've paid a lot for their grace and spiritual louts who've cheated on the price. As I've said several times now, grace has no price — it's *free*. End of subject.

FRANK: But isn't there a sense in which some responses to the reconciling grace we've already received are more fitting than others?

ROBERT: Yes. But "fitting" has too "worksy" a ring to it for my taste. I'd prefer to say that some responses are more *congruent* with grace than others. As a matter of fact, I granted that when I was talking to George. And I'll even grant you, Frank, that hell is a condition of *totally noncongruent* response to grace — a choosing of our own, nonexistent version of reality over God's freely given, reconciled version of it. But I still think the use of commercial language like "cheap" and "costly" is too easily misconstrued to be useful, and so I still think the subject should be ended.

ENID: Me too. So let's head for the real end.

ROBERT: All right. I think I've already said most of what I wanted to say at length. Let me simply give you a "shopping list" of the items I've set out to cover in this book. That way, you'll be able to check both my performance and your recollection.

1. The Mystery of Christ is none other than the *Mystery of the Incarnation* of the Word of God — of the Eternal Son, the Second Person of the Holy and Undivided Trinity.

2. The Mystery of Christ is indeed a *mystery:* it is a hidden fact of the universe that can only be *believed (trusted);* it cannot be directly known by, or proved to, our intellects.

3. Nevertheless, the Mystery of Christ has been *revealed* to us

in the Bible generally; and above all, it has been specifically *sacramentalized* — made *really present for us historically* in Jesus of Nazareth and in the church's witness by Word and Sacrament to the presence of our risen and ascended Lord Jesus Christ.

4. Those specific, historical sacramentalizations notwith-standing, however, the Mystery of Christ is a *cosmic, catholic* mystery, intimately and immediately *present* by the power of God *to all places, all times, and all people;* it is not the property of the church, nor is it confined to the church — and it is not in any way a localized phenomenon that extends itself only to those individuals who have made a transactional response to it.

5. Therefore, far from being a merely metaphysical truth or mystical perception, the Mystery of Christ is the *action of a Person doing something* (namely, making a New Creation) *in and for us.* It's not simply something to be discovered by speculation or inner experience; it's the *presence* of Some-one who is there for us regardless of what we believe, think, or feel.

6. Consequently, the Mystery of Christ has more than just an "existence" we might debate; it has a *Name* — and that Name, we believe as Christians, is JESUS.

7. And so, to conclude, JESUS, as the Word of God Incarnate, is *our life* — yours, mine, and the whole world's; we dwell in him and he dwells in us, and he is the Joy of all our Desiring.

There! I think that about sums it up. Now it's your turn. Why don't each of you think for a minute about everything we've said in this group and then give me a one- or two-sentence summary of your reaction to it. Who'll go first? Ah! Louise!

LOUISE: Frankly, I enjoyed the actual conversations with the people you counseled more than our discussions of them. Lots of times, I just got lost in the theology of it all.

ALICE: Well, I have to say I've learned a good deal and had some of my assumptions pretty heavily revised. It hasn't always been easy, but I thank you for the experience.

FRANK: You've challenged some of my assumptions too. And on a few of them, you've actually gotten through to me. But I still feel uneasy about how "relaxed" you make it all sound.

ENID: I think the whole experience has been great. As far as I'm concerned, you've taken orthodoxy and, without seriously compromising it in any way, relieved it of the transactional, nonmystical burden it's been saddled with for too long. Thank you for introducing us to the Mystery of Christ.

OTTO: I love arguments, so without any qualifications at all I can say I loved every minute of it. But now it's your turn, Robert. What do you have to say to such a mixed bag of reactions?

ROBERT: Good!

OTTO: That's all?

ROBERT: If you recall, that's all I ever say. If it was good enough for God at the end of each day in the first chapter of Genesis, it's good enough for me. In fact, I'll even add what he said at the end of the sixth day as my own parting shot:

Thank you all.
It's been VERY GOOD!

195